M000217181

ONE-TO-ONE **PERSONALIZATION** IN THE AGE OF **MACHINE LEARNING**

Harnessing Data to Power Great Customer Experiences

BY KARL WIRTH AND KATIE SWEET

EVERGAGE, INC.

*To all the incredible Evergage employees and customers
who are making the one-to-one dream a reality.*

Direction and Editing: Andy Zimmerman
Project Management: Paula Crerar
Design: Carol Chu, Ashton Landry and Courtney Vermette
Copyediting (first edition): Kylah Goodfellow Klinge
Additional Contributors: Greg Hinkle, Cliff Lyon, Jordan Bentley,
T.J. Prebil, Noah Sweet and the Evergage team

Second Edition
ISBN: 978-0-9993694-4-9

eISBN: 978-0-9993694-5-6

Printed in the United States of America

TABLE OF CONTENTS

KARL WIRTH

Karl is the CEO and Co-founder of Evergage, which provides the market-leading real-time personalization and customer data platform. Together with Greg Hinkle, Evergage's CTO, Karl founded Evergage in 2010 with the vision of building the next generation customer experience platform—one that not only collected and analyzed data but acted on it in the moment. Today, Evergage provides this solution, along with expert strategy and guidance, enabling hundreds of leading companies to realize the dream of one-to-one personalization. Prior to Evergage, Karl spent 10 years as a product and marketing innovator at several leading companies including RSA Security and Red Hat. He led the development of next-gen software businesses in security, cloud computing and marketing technology. Karl graduated from Harvard with a degree in Physics, and is the proud husband of Elizabeth Wirth and the father of four awesome kids.

KATIE SWEET

Katie is the Director of Content Marketing at Evergage. With a background in content and product marketing, she is responsible for creating content, managing and writing for the Evergage blog, and sharing the one-to-one vision with the world. She is a frequent writer on a variety of digital marketing and personalization topics. Katie holds an MBA from the D'Amore-McKim School of Business at Northeastern University, and she can often be found reading, traveling and trying adventurous foods.

WHY YOU SHOULD CARE ABOUT PERSONALIZATION

Ever since I started working in the professional world, I've needed to buy new suits and dress clothes about every six months. I would always go to a department store and wander around becoming increasingly frustrated. I didn't know the current trends or the inventory and, frankly, didn't want to invest the time to get to know them. I had a hard time selecting and matching fashionable clothes. Furthermore, even though I'd been shopping in the same store for years, the sales associates couldn't easily help me because they didn't know anything about me. I was on my own, wasting my time, and limiting my selections to basic blues and greens.

Fast-forward to several years ago when, for my birthday, my wife gave me an appointment with a personal shopper, Phillip, at a different department store. Now, about every six months, I call Phillip and tell him what I need. He knows what I have in my wardrobe, and he knows what I like. He also knows what's in stock, the styles that are trending and the sizes I wear. He considers my preferences in the context of the current styles, available inventory, and what other men like me are buying in order to pick out shirts, suits and ties that look good together and complement what I already have. Nowadays, when I go to the store to try on what Philip has selected, I typically leave with much more than I had planned on purchasing. Without a doubt, this is due to the great experience I had!

What's the main difference between my previously frustrating shopping trips and the enjoyable ones I now experience? Personalization. Personalization is the act of tailoring an experience or communication based on information a company has learned about a person. No one at the original store knew anything about me, so they couldn't tailor my experience (it was unpleasant and unproductive as a result). Phillip, on the other hand, got to know me, and he makes my shopping experience easy and painless by tailoring it to my needs and tastes.

Today, that level of personalization isn't just achievable in a store with a personal shopper. Technology now allows us to personalize the digital experience too—down to the individual level.

Here's an example. My primary bank, where I have my main credit card and mortgage, proactively reached out to me with an email about refinancing and home equity loans. The email directed me to a landing page where I found information that got me to consider one of these offers. Later in the day, I went back to the site. It showed no knowledge of me. It didn't mention loans or rates. I even went back to the site several times over the week as I comparison-shopped other banks. Eventually I took out a loan with one of those other banks. What could my bank have done differently?

The bank could have paid attention to what I was doing—perusing the site for home equity line options, risks and rewards. I even put my information into the site's calculator (how much clearer could I have been about my intent?!), but it didn't take that data into consideration and turn it into an opportunity to talk to me in a personalized manner. It could have closed the sale by recognizing me and my intentions, guiding me to the information I needed, and highlighting the reasons I should do business with that bank instead of going elsewhere.

When marketers think of personalization, they tend to associate the idea with certain major online brands, such as Amazon, Netflix and Spotify. They assume that personalization is out of reach for smaller companies with fewer resources. But the reality is that consumers are getting this type of personalized experience from a wide range of companies across channels. Consumers are beginning to expect that level of personalization from almost all of the companies they interact with, regardless of industry.

Think about your life as a consumer. How many times has your bank communicated to you about a product you already have? How many times have you received an email from one of your favorite retailers announcing a sale in a category you've never shopped (like baby clothes if you're not a parent or lawn care when you live in a high-rise apartment)? In your work life, how many times have you gone to a company's website and been shown a video you've already seen, targeted to an industry that isn't yours? Once you become accustomed to personalization, these become glaring mistakes. And even though these are simple examples, it's at moments like these that you realize these companies don't really know you, even when you're a regular customer! And if they don't know you, they don't really deserve your loyalty.

Personalization is the direction the world is heading. That's not a prediction—it's a fact. We're seeing it now. It is currently impacting our lives as consumers, and it will increasingly become an imperative for marketers as time goes on. This is the reason I co-founded Evergage: to make it easy for businesses to realize this imperative.

In this book, we describe the past, present and future of personalization. We provide tips on how to get started with the right people, processes, technologies and strategies for a forward-looking marketing strategy. We outline the different data types involved in personalization and highlight the important role a customer data platform (CDP) can play in consolidating and synthesizing relevant customer data. And most importantly, we describe how critical machine learning is for the modern marketer. I hope that the book will give you a strong foundation to incorporate personalization into your marketing customer experience strategies and successfully prepare you for a personalized future.

—Karl

THE EVOLUTION OF THE INTERNET TOWARD PERSONALIZATION

Imagine you're considering an upgrade to your kitchen. A kitchen remodel is a big project—one you're not likely to undertake without substantial research. So, before you make any serious plans, you probably want to check out a few home improvement sites for some inspiration.

After you've invested significant time on one of those sites, that site should have a good idea of what you're looking for and of your general preferences. It should be able to recognize that you're primarily interested in ovens, for example, and that since you also researched other appliances, you're likely planning a remodel. It should detect that you're most interested in stainless steel and gain an understanding of your preferred price range.

Most importantly, the site should be able to leverage all of this information about you to subtly personalize your experience. The product and category recommendations across the site should reflect your preferences. The search results and the way those results are ordered should reflect your preferences. The navigation of the site should reflect your preferences. Articles and buying guides relevant to home remodeling should be surfaced for you. And your whole experience should become more and more relevant as you continue to engage with the site.

Sounds great, right? Well, it can get even more impressive. If you ultimately decide to visit the store in person to talk to an expert about your remodel, the in-store staff should be familiar with your preferences so they can help and continue to recommend items to you. And any future communication with you, such as emails or call center interactions, should draw from the same information the site collects.

Once you've experienced this level of service, any non-personalized experience falls flat. You may not be able to recognize that a lack of personalization is the reason for a lackluster experience, but you'll feel that any other home improvement company isn't relevant to you, or that it's too hard to find what you're looking for. You may feel that the retailer has too many product options and that the experience just seems overwhelming.

That feeling of frustration is what drives people away from certain companies and toward those that better understand them. It is why personalization is so important. Right now, the level of personalization described above is indeed possible, and it is a competitive advantage to those companies that are providing it. But in the future, it will be table stakes for operating any business. Any site, email, app, or store clerk that fails to provide a highly personalized experience will be at a disadvantage. So it's time to invest in personalization now.

How do we know that this is the way the world is headed? All you have to do is look at history. Before we describe how to achieve this level of one-to-one interaction with your customers, let's take a brief step back in time.

THE PRE-INTERNET ERA

Before the Industrial Revolution ushered in a new age of mass production, most businesses were local stores. As a proprietor of such a store, you knew all of your customers well. You knew how often they visited the store, what they bought, and what their home lives were like. This information would reside in your head, and you'd use it to help each and every shopper who would walk through your door. The approach allowed for an extraordinary level of personalization, but it wasn't scalable.

When mass production took hold, mass marketing was the name of the game. Appealing to the largest swath of people with a singular product was the goal. Leveraging mass media, you could reach those consumers in newspapers and print ads, on the radio and billboards, and eventually on television—in very large numbers. The more people your product appealed to, and the more people you could reach with a message for the lowest common denominator, the larger the size of your market. This approach is the complete opposite of the local store experience—extremely scalable, but not at all personal.

THE DAWN OF THE INTERNET AGE

Technology started to transform the landscape in the early 1990s. The term "one-to-one marketing" was first introduced in 1993 and was formally articulated in the book *The One to One Future,* by Don Peppers and Martha Rogers.[1] In the book, Peppers and Rogers describe the shift they were beginning to see from a focus on "share of market" to "share of customer." They emphasized that we were headed into an era where mass marketing would no longer be an effective way to compete. They predicted that "using the new media of the one-to-one future, you will be able to communicate directly with consumers, individually, rather than shouting at them, in groups."[2]

One of the biggest differences between a "share of customer" and a "share of market" approach should be obvious—knowledge of the customer. After all, customer information is a key differentiating factor between the local store experience and the mass-marketed approach. Peppers and Rogers note that:

> *The key share-of-customer requirement is to know your cus-*
> *tomers 1:1... You must know who your loyal customers are, so*

you can take steps to make sure that yours is the brand they choose even more often.

… Today's mass-marketing paradigm has no need for interactive media and computers that track individual customer transactions linked over time. Tracking customers and conversing with them individually are not tasks that fit into a market-share approach to competition.[3]

Peppers and Rogers theorized that having large quantities of data at the individual level would be a competitive differentiator for businesses as the industry evolved to a more relationship-driven world.[4]

While Peppers and Rogers demonstrated incredible foresight in their predictions of a one-to-one future, there were two key challenges with one-to-one marketing in the early '90s. First, the type of individualized data they described was extremely hard to come by, let alone act on quickly. Most of the consumer data available to marketers came from surveys of attitudes and stated intentions statistically projected to the population as a whole. This type of data is helpful for understanding trends at the segment level (such as how young, affluent consumers feel about eco-friendly products), but it isn't useful in a one-to-one capacity.

The second challenge marketers in the '90s faced was that the channel with the largest potential for one-to-one interactions—the internet—had not reached its full potential. Peppers and Rogers themselves struggled to grasp what, exactly, would be possible with the internet. Their visions of one-to-one marketing tended to remain in the realm of direct mail, phone calls and voicemails, and "facsimile machines." For advice on how to provide personalized experiences online, they had this to share:

Give your 'visitors' the opportunity and incentive to let you know who they are. Tag them, if possible, so you will know them when they next visit your site. Think of all the ways you can continue to customize your communications and offers to them individually.

If your firm has a major investment in Web communications, you have no excuse for not taking full advantage of the latest customization capabilities made possible by companies such as BroadVision. This West Coast firm can actually dynamically customize your Web page, based on whether and how a visitor has used it previously. A user who came to your site and expressed an interest in a particular baseball team, for instance, could see a 'hot button' for a chat group of that team's fans when he comes to your site for his next visit.[5]

The company they mention, BroadVision, was founded around the time *The One to One Future* was published. BroadVisions's One-to-One software was positioned to help companies profile website visitors and use that information to tailor marketing messages to the individual. The company was described in a Stanford case study a few years after its founding as "well positioned to become the leading supplier of enterprise-class solutions for personalized, one-to-one business on the Internet."[6] While BroadVision marketed its solution as "one-to-one," it only allowed marketers to leverage simple rules to personalize small parts of their websites to broad segments. Although impressive for its time, it was clearly a far cry from the one-to-one experiences we described earlier in this chapter.

Peppers and Rogers can't be faulted for their lack of specifics around how one-to-one marketing could extend to the internet. At the time, e-commerce was in its infancy (Amazon didn't get its start as a bookseller until 1994), and only 23% of US households had a computer—never mind internet access.[7]

Reading Peppers and Rogers' book in 1994 must have been a fascinating peek into the internet's possible future. George Gendron of *Inc. Magazine* wrote about the work, "This is not the book of the year. It's not even the book of a decade. It's one of the two or three most important business books written."[8] It must have opened marketers' eyes to what personalization could someday mean—and to what clearly wasn't possible yet.

THE ROOTS OF PERSONALIZATION

In 1999, journalists were already commenting that the one-to-one dream wasn't yet a reality and that the vast majority of websites were still treating everyone the same. Amazon, of course, was cited as the leader of the pack. In 1999, five years after Amazon was founded, owner Jeff Bezos was named *Time* magazine's "Man of the Year." Amazon, and Bezos specifically, was credited with popularizing e-commerce.[9]

Although Amazon's product recommendations created the standard for personalization, other tech companies were quickly springing up to cater to the newly popular e-commerce market. One such company, LikeMinds, founded in 1997, developed recommendations using an important algorithmic method called collaborative filtering (which we'll discuss again later in the book). It allowed marketers to deliver personalized recommendations based on clickstream data, purchase history and product similarities. In the early stages of its existence, LikeMinds' recommendations primarily leveraged explicit data, such as preferences that were directly solicited from visitors.[10]

Some early examples of one-to-one marketing came out of this era. Toyota used BroadVision to create a dynamic car-building experience on its site. Visitors could volunteer lifestyle information to Toyota and then configure their own cars on the site. They also could save their cars and return to them later. Similarly, Levi's asked visitors to answer a few questions about their preferences in looks, music and other forms of entertainment. LikeMinds used this explicit data to deliver personalized product recommendations.[11]

It's worth noting that during this era, "one-to-one" was being attributed to two different tactics we apply today: personalization and customization. Today we say that a website is **personalized** when it tailors itself to the visitor based on data it has collected (such as past behavior, known attributes, etc.). **Customization,** on the other hand, occurs when visitors intentionally modify their own experiences.

Currently, when you adjust your Gmail settings to indicate the number of messages you want per page and add a signature, you are customizing your email experience. But when Gmail displays advertisements to you based on your interests, it's personalizing your experience for you. In the first example, you're intentionally changing the experience. In the second, you're receiving more relevant ads without taking any action yourself.

In the late '90s, tools like BroadVision and LikeMinds were used to both personalize and customize, and both approaches were described as "one-to-one." For personalization, BroadVision could leverage simple business rules (like in the "hot button" chat room example Peppers and Rogers cited). LikeMinds could provide product recommendations based on what "others like you" also shopped. While not technically one-to-one (more like one-to-many), these tactics are still a form of personalization.

Yet the Toyota and Levi's examples are more aligned with what we consider customization today. Visitors to Toyota's site were able to customize and store their own virtual cars in their profiles, while Levi's shoppers were able to customize their shopping experience by providing information about themselves. These early one-to-one attempts were valuable, but it's worth making the distinction that they weren't necessarily the type of one-to-one personalization that we think of today.

THE EMERGENCE OF REAL-TIME WEB ANALYTICS

Fast-forward to the late 2000s, roughly 15 years after the introduction of e-commerce and Peppers and Rogers' dream of one-to-one, and we still hadn't achieved true one-to-one personalization. Peppers and Rogers wrote in a follow-up white paper that while a lot of progress had been made since 1994, they believed that the business world was still on its one-to-one journey.[12]

At this point, the major impact that the internet would have on one-to-one customer interactions was certainly clear. While only 18% of US households had internet access in 1997, by 2009 that number had grown to 74%.[13] Meanwhile, the 2008 financial crisis made the relationship-driven experiences that strengthened loyalty among existing customers even more critical.[14]

During this period, a technological advancement central to one-to-one personalization emerged: real-time analytics. While the importance of consumer data was established in the early '90s, the industry was realizing that the ability to access analytics in **real time** was absolutely essential to one-to-one customer interactions.

Web analytics began with log files in 1993. At that point, every time someone visited a website, the browser made an HTTP request to the site's server to load every item on the page. Since most websites were made up of only one static page of content, a single hit to the server represented one page view.[15] A record of all of these requests was stored in the log file, but it contained a lot of data and was complicated to decipher. As a result, site data was often the responsibility of a company's IT department, and it was used primarily to understand site performance.[16]

Some tools did crop up to make these log files easier to interpret by a company's marketing team, such as WebTrends and Analog.[17] In 1995, a company called Web Depot was founded. While it was originally a web consultancy, it moved into web analytics when the team realized that their product, called Urchin, could process log files in only 15 minutes—as opposed to the 24 hours that was common at the time.[18]

Yet log files became harder to interpret as the internet evolved. Browsers developed the ability to cache—storing a version of a file in the browser so it did not need to make a call to the server if a page was loaded multiple times. As a result, visits that involved caching did not appear in the log file. Additionally, web pages became more complex to contain multiple files (such as images and videos), so multiple requests had to be made to a server to load every element of the page. This severely complicated the log files.[19]

Javascript tags overcame some of these challenges starting in 1997. Javascript-based analytics is based on URLs and cookies. A cookie generally represents one person, so Javascript tagging remains an easier way to understand an individual's path through a site.[20] At this time, Urchin, while still predominantly log-based, added a product called Urchin On Demand that leveraged Javascript tagging.[21]

In 2005, Urchin was bought by Google. Urchin On Demand became the foundation of Google Analytics (while log-based Urchin was phased out), and Javascript tagging remains the dominant method for web analytics today.[22] Of course, these days Google Analytics is a dominant player in the web analytics industry, along with Omniture (now Adobe Analytics, which is part of Adobe Marketing Cloud).

The evolution described above led to the development of real-time data in the late 2000s. Patric Timmermans, director of CRM at Infor in 2008, captured the spirit of the age—and its limitations:

Customer dialogue has become the most important manifestation of one-to-one marketing. Companies used to cheer about having updated data every six weeks. Then they felt great about updating customer data every week. Now we've progressed to the point where companies can have constantly updated customer information, but I don't think enough companies understand exactly how important real-time customer information can be.[23]

One-to-one personalization requires more than the collection of data: that data needs to be actionable. According to Timmermans, the capabilities were there to access real-time customer data, but marketers weren't certain about what to do with that data. So while real-time data was available in the late 2000s, the data was not quite ready for use in real-time personalization. And, of course, technology was still evolving to include more and more channels that complicated the one-to-one vision. Notably, the first iPhone was released in 2007, but most marketers had not yet thought about collecting data from mobile browsing. Clearly, there was more work to be done.

ONE-TO-ONE TODAY

Looking back at all this history, it's clear that we've made great progress. But this progress has been slow. One-to-one marketing was envisaged in 1993. Today, how many marketers could honestly say that they're delivering the kind of truly personalized, one-to-one experiences described at the beginning of this chapter? We've spoken to many marketers, and from our experience we can confidently say that the answer remains "not many."

What happened to the technology providers that were spearheading the one-to-one revolution? BroadVision is still around, but it's fallen a long way since its heyday in the '90s. Today it is primarily focused on workplace collaboration and portal solutions, having "pivoted" after the dotcom bubble collapsed.[24] LikeMinds was acquired by IBM in the early 2000s[25] and is still currently marketed for e-commerce recommendations.

But today, the biggest name in personalization is Adobe, which has made personalization a core aspect of its Adobe Marketing Cloud. The truth, however, is that while Adobe preaches a vision of one-to-one interactions, its solution to deliver on that vision is lacking. It comprises an assortment of products pieced together from various acquisitions. They have major functionality gaps, are not well-integrated, and are complicated to implement and operate. Key components were built long ago without real-time or big data in mind. These are not architectural oversights that can be easily fixed.

We frequently encounter marketers whose experiences with Adobe have led them to believe that fully personalized, real-time, one-to-one experiences are beyond their reach. They think: *If the market leader can't enable me to do it, it must not be possible.* And who can blame them? They've been hearing for decades that one-to-one marketing is within reach, when it clearly hasn't been.

If you're struggling with personalization today, perhaps it's because you've been unable to execute a personalization strategy at scale, or that you haven't even tried because it seems too difficult to accomplish.

Personalization has come a long way since it was first introduced in the early '90s, and it will, of course, continue to advance. (We'll provide some predictions for the future in the last chapter of this book.) But there's already so much that can be done today at the one-to-one level with existing technology.

In the rest of the book, we describe what you need to be truly successful with one-to-one personalization today and over the next decade. In brief, achieving the one-to-one vision requires:

- Advanced machine-learning algorithms that can synthesize large amounts of data in real time and deliver individualized experiences *(Chapter 2: Machine Learning is Changing the Game)*

- A cross-channel approach with a focus on reaching people with individualized experiences, regardless of where they engage with the brand or company (*Chapter 3: Think Bigger, Think Cross-Channel*)
- The ability to track deep behavioral data on each individual and to combine it with other sources of customer data with the assistance of a customer data platform (*Chapter 4: Garbage In, Garbage Out*)
- A view of one-to-one personalization as a key component of your marketing strategy and customer experience, not an afterthought (*Chapter 5: Consider the Full Experience*)
- Analytics and measurement that are just as sophisticated as your data and personalization campaigns (*Chapter 6: Testing, Analytics and ROI*)
- The right strategy to make one-to-one personalization work for your own business (*Chapter 7: Planning for Personalization*)
- The right technology to implement your strategy (*Chapter 8: Finding the Right Tech for the Job*)
- A look to the future to stay on top of quickly evolving trends (*Chapter 9: The Future of Personalization*)

Together, these essential components—covered in the remaining chapters—will enable you to execute your one-to-one vision.

CHAPTER 1 ENDNOTES

1. Infor, Peppers & Rogers Group, "The One-to-One Future: Are We There Yet," 2008, http://www.agentsdirectmail.com/marketing/one-to-one_future.pdf.

2. Don Peppers and Martha Rogers, The One to One Future. (New York: Doubleday, 1993) p. 10.

3. Ibid, p. 19.

4. Ibid, p. 138-139.

5. Ibid, p. 241.

6. Stanford case study, "BroadVision," Mar 1998.

7. US Census Bureau, "Home Computers and Internet Use in the United States: August 2000," Sep 2001.

8. Don Peppers and Martha Rogers. The One to One Future. (New York: Doubleday, 1993), front cover.

9. Wired.com, "Man of the Year: Jeff Bezos," Dec 1999.

10. Campaignlive.co.uk, "The Web Tomorrow - Do you still believe in one-to-one marketing?" May 1999, http://www.campaignlive.co.uk/article/web-tomorrow-believe-one-to-one-marketing/121855#V4e4yAoKwqP5ygOV.99.

11. Ibid.

12. Infor, Peppers & Rogers Group, "The One-to-One Future: Are We There Yet," 2008, http://www.agentsdirectmail.com/marketing/one-to-one_future.pdf.

13. US Census Bureau, "Computer and Internet Use in the United States," May 2013, https://www.census.gov/library/publications/2013/demo/p20-569.html.

14. Infor, Peppers & Rogers Group, "The One-to-One Future: Are We There Yet," 2008.

15. Clicktale, "A brief history of web analytics," Nov 2010, https://www.clicktale.com/resources/blog/a-brief-history-of-web-analytics/.

16. Amplitude, "The Early Days of Web Analytics," https://amplitude.com/blog/2015/06/15/the-early-days-of-web-analytics/.

17. Clicktale, "A brief history of web analytics," Nov 2010, https://www.clicktale.com/resources/blog/a-brief-history-of-web-analytics/.

18. Celine Roque, "The Real Story on How Google Analytics Got Started," Attendly.com, Apr 2013, http://www.attendly.com/the-real-story-on-how-google-analytics-got-started/.

19. Amplitude, "The Early Days of Web Analytics," https://amplitude.com/blog/2015/06/15/the-early-days-of-web-analytics/.

20. Gordon Choi, "Web Analytics: JavaScript vs. Web Log," ClickZ.com, Jul 2012, https://www.clickz.com/web-analytics-javascript-vs-web-log/38343/.

21. Celine Roque, "The Real Story on How Google Analytics Got Started," Attendly.com, Apr 2013, http://www.attendly.com/the-real-story-on-how-google-analytics-got-started/.

22. Ibid.

23. Infor, Peppers & Rogers Group, "The One-to-One Future: Are We There Yet," 2008, http://www.agentsdirectmail.com/marketing/one-to-one_future.pdf.

24. Cathleen Santosus, "BroadVision at the Crossroads," ecommercetimes.com, Nov 2002, http://www.ecommercetimes.com/story/19945.html.

25. Brian Lesser, Programming Flash Communication Server, 2005, p. xii.

CHAPTER 2

MACHINE LEARNING IS CHANGING THE GAME

As the title suggests, machine learning is truly revolutionizing marketing at the one-to-one level. Before we delve into what that revolution looks like, let's define some terms. Many marketers we've spoken to are confused by the industry's inability to settle on a clear definition for "machine learning," and there is frequent confusion between that phrase and "artificial intelligence" (AI). In these definitions, note that artificial intelligence is the broader field that includes machine learning (as well as other areas, such as speech recognition), and that computer science is the broader field that includes AI:

Computer science: The study of the principles and use of computers. It's a broad category that encompasses such areas as software engineering, computer networks, computer security, and artificial intelligence.[26]

Artificial intelligence: The theory and development of computer systems able to perform tasks that normally require human intelligence, such as visual perception, speech recognition, translation between languages and design-making.[27]

Machine learning: Programming computers to make intelligent decisions—and to draw conclusions—without human involvement. Machine learning has broad applicability across fields, but in the context of personalization, it is used to make the best decision about which experience or engagement to show each person at the one-to-one level.

With the terms defined, we can now turn our attention back to personalization. In this chapter, we'll review the two main types of personalization: rule-based and machine-learning personalization. We'll also take a brief look at predictive segments, a sort of hybrid that uses machine learning to automatically put people into different groups, or "clusters," in order to reduce the effort associated with rule-based personalization.

To elucidate these personalization types, let's return to that example Peppers and Rogers gave for website personalization back in 1994. They wrote: "A user who came to your site and expressed an interest in a particular baseball team, for instance, could see a 'hot button' for a chat group of that team's fans when he comes to your site for his next visit." We would probably call that "hot button" a call-to-action (CTA) button today, and we wouldn't have to wait for the person's next visit to personalize his experience or require him to "express" an interest for it to be determined, inferred or deduced. Nevertheless, the use case is still valid.

Let's say you work for a tech company, and in the hero section atop your homepage, you have a CTA that invites your site's visitor to "Explore Solutions." If the visitor is in the healthcare industry, you could modify that CTA to say "Explore Healthcare Solutions." Clicking the link would send him to a page related to health and medicine, while any visitor not in the healthcare industry would see something different.

In this example, you would use a rule to implement the campaign: *If visitor is in healthcare, show the healthcare experience.* Rules provide marketers with a simple way to personalize an experience. They are extremely useful and will probably always be employed in some capacity for personalization, but they are not typically applied to one-to-one communication. That is where machine learning comes in. Although BroadVision claimed to offer "one-to-one marketing" in the '90s, its rule-based system did not actually allow for scalable one-to-one communication. The same holds true for rule-based personalization today.

RULE-BASED PERSONALIZATION

Rule-based personalization allows marketers to deliver experiences and engagement to specific groups or segments of people based on the manual creation and manipulation of business rules. As our definition suggests, segments form the foundation of rule-based personalization. Segments allow you to categorize a subset of your prospects and customers according to their attributes and behaviors. You then use rules to tailor the experience for each segment.

The simplest way to think about rule-based personalization is in the form of IF/THEN statements: *IF a person falls into segment A, THEN show him experience X.*

For example:
> *IF a visitor is located in Los Angeles,*
> *THEN send her an email, push notification or ad about an event in the LA area.*

> *IF a visitor is a member of your loyalty program,*
> *THEN change the hero area to address a returning customer.*

Segments can be broad or narrow. A segment created using just one or two data points would be considered a broad segment, which means that many individuals will fit into it. For example, an online apparel retailer can personalize its website according to its visitors' geolocations, showing everyone in a certain region the clothing and footwear appropriate for that climate. A B2B site could email customers with industry-specific case studies. In these examples, many people are likely to fit into the segments and will therefore receive the same experience.

Segments that begin to combine multiple data points are narrow segments. They often leverage nested "AND" and "OR" logic to identify very specific groups of visitors. For instance, the clothing retailer could recognize a repeat visitor from Florida who originated from a specific ad campaign and point him to the "sun-lovers" sale merchandise with which he engaged in the past. The B2B tech company site could recognize prospects from the financial services industry who have already spent a certain amount of time exploring particular product pages, such as network servers, and email a relevant white paper. In these cases, the size of the segment will be much smaller—because fewer people will fit the criteria.

Marketers must decide for themselves whether the effort to design an experience for a very small group of people is worthwhile. In some instances, doing so will be fruitful. For example, if you're implementing an account-based marketing (ABM) strategy, you want to create highly tailored communications to reach specific accounts. However, most marketers probably don't want to set up rules to speak to individuals at the one-to-one level.

CASE STUDY: DYN

Dyn, a cloud-based Internet Performance Management (IPM) company, has two major product categories targeted to two different audiences: enterprise and small business/consumer. Enterprise audiences are encouraged to fill out a form on the website to speak with a salesperson, while small business/consumer audiences are able to purchase products directly from the site.

Due to the priorities of the business, enterprise solutions were given the majority of the real estate in the navigation

Dyn uses a rule to show small business/consumer segment this slimmed-down version of the navigation menu.

menu, while personal and small business solutions were given a smaller corner of the navigation. The e-commerce team feared that small business visitors who came to the site may not notice that corner in the navigation and assume that Dyn was not a good fit for them.

The team needed a way to show small businesses and consumers that Dyn was relevant to their needs, but not at the expense of the company's enterprise business. Dyn used rule-based personalization to modify the site's navigation menu in real time when a small business visitor landed on the site. The company created a segment of small business/consumer visitors based on particular referring URLs or originating referrer search terms, previous visits to specific product pages, and/or previously purchased products.

When anyone from the small business/consumer segment is on the site, a simple rule dynamically modifies the site navigation to display a more relevant experience for that group. These visitors see a slimmed-down version of the menu, with small business/consumer products prominently displayed. All the enterprise links are still accessible to these visitors in a new tab in the navigation called "Enterprise." Meanwhile, the original navigation is still shown to all other visitors who don't fall into the small business/consumer segment.

With this subtle personalization of the site navigation, Dyn experienced a 20% increase in average order value and a 7% increase in conversion rate for its e-commerce products—with no negative impact to its enterprise solutions.

The Dyn case study is an example of a company significantly improving its average order value and conversion rate with a single personalization campaign. Remarkably, it was able to create this experience using just one simple segment and one rule. The company's modest campaign made a considerable difference.

But let's say it wanted to do more to personalize its navigation. Assume it wanted to highlight products that small business or enterprise visitors had engaged with most while on the site, and it wanted to order the content under the "Resources" tab to focus on the resources that a visitor had not yet viewed. This type of personalization is possible with rules, and the right personalization solution would make it possible to add, manage and prioritize rules to achieve this objective.

But the more rules you add, the more complicated everything becomes. Personalizing at the individual level in just that small section of Dyn's site would require several rules. To personalize the rest of the site, the company would need to set up and manage hundreds or even thousands of rules. That's just not scalable. It's easy to lose track of numerous campaigns running in parallel. If something breaks, troubleshooting becomes incredibly difficult and time-consuming—not to mention the effort required to build all of those rules and design the corresponding experiences.

That said, under the right circumstances, the use of dynamic variables—a more scalable form of rule-based personalization—can help simplify certain rule-based campaigns. If Dyn had wanted to cater more to their enterprise prospects, for example, perhaps specifically targeting their top 150 strategic accounts as part of its ABM strategy, they could present them with a relevant, personalized welcome message and a call-to-action with dynamic variables. Instead of setting up 150 individual campaigns with 150 rules, they could implement one campaign that filled in the name of the account as a variable.

While rules are well-suited to the type of segment-based personalization that Dyn uses in its site navigation, this approach is far less suited to one-to-one personalization. That type of personalization is much more achievable with machine-learning algorithms, which we'll get to shortly.

PREDICTIVE SEGMENTS (AUTOMATIC CLUSTERING)

As we mentioned at the beginning of this chapter and will describe in more depth in the next section, machine learning has revolutionized the way we deliver one-to-one personalization intelligently and at scale. Yet it is important to point out that machine learning is also revolutionizing the speed, scale and depth of data analysis to yield invaluable insights. For example, machine learning can be used to identify groups or clusters of visitors with similar behaviors and affinities (called "predictive segments" or "automatic clustering"). This algorithmic technique highlights the differences in conversion and behavioral statistics between clusters to enable more relevant insights and targeting—essentially allowing marketers to create smarter segments more quickly and easily.

The application of machine learning offers two key benefits:

UNCOVERING AND ACTING ON DIFFERENCES BETWEEN SEGMENTS

Machine learning can help you identify differences in behaviors among your existing segments that may not be easy to identify from a manual inspection of the data. For example, what are the key differences in behavior between a customer who churns versus one who stays? What are the attributes and behaviors of a high-value customer or prospect who converts versus low-value customers or prospects who don't convert? With those insights, you can react more quickly to business trends and create new opportunities to advance your business.

For example, you could create a "churn risk" segment or a "potential high-value customer" segment and include people who exhibit behaviors similar to customers who did churn in the first case or to existing high-value customers in the second. Using these segments, you can then create appropriate personalized experiences through digital and physical channels to encourage high churn risks to stay and potential high-value customers to purchase.

DISCOVERING AND ACTING ON NEW SEGMENTS OF INTEREST

When segmenting your visitors, customers, prospects or shoppers, the value of some segments is obvious. Yet there are likely other valuable audiences that are not obvious to you initially but become apparent in the data. You might find, for example, that prospects with an affinity for one category or product end up converting at a much higher rate than do others. Or you might discover that visitors who read case studies on your site tend to be further down the purchase funnel for your solution. Automatic clustering can yield these insights and identify groups whom you can then target with relevant, personalized experiences.

Predictive segmentation enables you to identify valuable segments of which you might otherwise be unaware and to learn what makes those segments unique. After all, it doesn't do you any good to create segments and target them with tailored experiences if you don't know if those are the best segments to target. Without that knowledge, you must rely on your best guesses about which and how various audiences will respond. Machine learning can take the guesswork out of segmentation.

MACHINE-LEARNING PERSONALIZATION: REALIZING THE ONE-TO-ONE DREAM

Now that we've described how rules can be used to target experiences to segments and how machine learning can be applied to segmentation, we can finally address how machine learning makes the dream of one-to-one personalization a reality. But first, let's put forth another important definition. **Machine-learning personalization** utilizes algorithms and predictive analytics to dynamically present the most relevant content or experience for each and every visitor and customer.

Essentially, machine-learning personalization provides a highly scalable way to provide unique experiences to your visitors and customers—all the way down to the individual level. Anything from recommending products, categories, brands, articles, promotions and offers, to dynamically modifying site navigation, search results and list sorting is possible with machine learning.

Popularized by household names like Amazon and Netflix, algorithms aren't just for giant e-commerce companies. They can be utilized by marketers from companies of any size and in any industry. And while slightly more complex to understand than rules, algorithms can be created and managed by marketers or other business users with the right solution.

Because one algorithm can do the work of thousands of rules, algorithms ultimately result in simpler deployments. So, if you wanted to personalize your site navigation to include the most relevant links for every visitor based on their behaviors and individual preferences—without building thousands of rules—you would use machine learning. Or in another example, if you wanted to send one batch email to the ten million customers in your loyalty program—yet still allow each email to contain relevant offers, content, and promotions—you would use machine learning.

To begin, it helps to understand what makes up a machine-learning algorithm. Assuming you're going to use a customizable algorithm—which you should—you would start by selecting one or more base algorithms. Apply filters to include or exclude specific variables. Add in boosters to account for individual preferences. Finally, determine whether you want to apply any variations.

We'll describe these elements of an algorithm in more depth below, using product or content recommendations for consistency.

But as we'll elucidate through the rest of the book, algorithms can be used for far more than recommendations.

BASE ALGORITHMS

Base algorithms are the foundation for delivering recommendations and individualized experiences and engagement. When choosing a base algorithm, you have the opportunity to tell the machine where to begin for selecting items to recommend. There are basic algorithms with which you might already be familiar, and more sophisticated algorithms that leverage advanced machine-learning principles.

BASIC ALGORITHMS

Basic algorithms generally rely on specific criteria or the "wisdom of the crowd." Some of the most common are:

Trending: Items are recommended based on what is most popular on the site during a specific time period.

Recently Published: Items are recommended based on what has recently been added to the site.

Soon to Expire: Recommended items are prioritized based on their upcoming expiration dates.

Co-Browse: Items are recommended based on what other people on the site have also viewed.

Co-Buy: Items are recommended based on what other people on the site have also purchased.

Similar Items: Items are recommended based on similarity in product type or category.

Different base algorithms are suited to different use cases. For example, a retailer may want to highlight trending or recently published items on the homepage, while promoting co-browse items on a product detail page (PDP)—or to do something else entirely. It all depends on the site's goals.

ADVANCED ALGORITHMS

Advanced algorithms are sophisticated and complex. While a basic algorithm would show Product X to everyone who looked at Product Y, for example, advanced algorithms *predict* the best experience for each individual, growing smarter over time as they have more data to leverage. Here are a few of the most common:

Collaborative Filtering: Based on a visitor's engagement with different items, he is grouped into a cluster of people with similar likes and dislikes. Items are then recommended by comparing him to others in his cluster. (Netflix, for example, uses this technique.)

Random Forest (Decision Trees): Detects the best converting paths, actions and content for influencing an individual's journey toward conversion. The algorithm then uses those paths to show him the correct right next step at the right time.

Contextual Bandit: Using explicit, known visitor data, this algorithm selects the best converting offers and promotions even before a user demonstrates interest through behavior. (We'll describe this algorithm in more detail in Chapter 6 when we discuss testing.)

Text Analysis: Utilizing Natural Language Processing (NLP), this algorithm determines the strongest keywords within the text-based content a visitor consumes and uses that language to affect a personalized experience.

A discussion of precisely how these algorithms operate is outside the scope of this book, but with the right solution, marketers can test and implement algorithms like these on their own. And the right approach, as we'll discuss, is often to combine multiple algorithms to form a custom, hybrid algorithm for a particular use case.

FILTERS

Many marketers are uncomfortable with the idea of handing over their digital experiences to a machine, and that is completely understandable. You likely know your products, content and categories well, and it can be unsettling to cede control of something so important. But you should never relinquish complete control. Choosing filters and other variables enables you to stay in charge.

After you've picked one or more base algorithms, you can customize them by including or excluding certain criteria using filters. Filters allow you to exercise control over the categories, brands, price ranges, locations and other attributes that are shown in your recommendations. In other words, you can add human guidance to your machine-learning-driven experiences.

There are many reasons to use filters. One reason is to use your knowledge of your business and products or content to deliver more helpful recommendations. For example, a retailer may want to use the recommendations on its product detail pages (PDPs) to help shoppers find other products in the same category. On a clothing site, for instance, the retailer may want shoppers browsing shoes to see recommendations only for other shoes. In that case, the retailer would apply a filter to *include* just that one category. Other retailers may decide to use PDP recommendations to drive upsells, such as recommending jewelry and other accessories to "complete the look" while a shopper is viewing a dress. In this case, the filter would *exclude* the category of the product being shown.

A B2B site focused on demand generation can leverage filters as well. Most demand generation sites have a lot of content assets, as well as many web pages across the site where they can recommend that content. On a web page that explains how the company serves the financial services industry, the marketing team can choose to include content (eBooks, case studies, blog posts, etc.) in the financial services category only. Or, assume the same B2B site has a thank you page after a prospect has registered for a webinar. The site's marketing team may want to feature a few relevant content assets for her to read after registering—to keep her engaged on the site rather than reach a dead-end page. The team may want to *exclude* webinars as a content type for that page (since she is already currently registered for one), and instead feature other asset types that she can peruse immediately.

You can also use filters to apply restrictions for business reasons. For example, a retailer may wish to exclude Brand A from the product pages of its rival, Brand B, due to the request of the manufacturer. In that case, products from Brand B will not be shown in recommendations on product pages for Brand A, or vice versa. A B2B site focused on demand generation may want to only include content recommendations for a specific topic or keyword in a few select areas of the site to align with company goals or marketing calendar. In that case, only content around a certain topic would be promoted at a certain time.

BOOSTERS

Next, boosting allows you to incorporate and prioritize the specific preferences in brand, category, price range, color, gender, content type, keyword, etc. of each individual on your site. These preferences can be determined with deep behavioral tracking on each individual—incorporating not just what a visitor clicks on, but also mouse movement, scrolling, inactivity and time spent per page— combined with all the other customer data you have available to give a clear indication of preference and level of interest. We'll cover this in more detail in Chapter 4.

When you're able to interpret all of your customer data, you can uncover the individual preferences and affinities of each person and use that information to "boost" the results of your algorithms and make them even more relevant at the one-to-one level. While advanced algorithms are already relevant at the one-to-one level, boosting allows you to individualize even basic algorithms.

There are many different ways in which boosters can be applied to completely individualize your experiences and recommendations. They can ensure that a person's favorite brands are prioritized across your site, that she sees recommendations within her preferred price range, or that she sees content related to her preferred topics or that aligns with her stage of the buyer's journey.

For example, if a shoe retailer selected a "trending" base algorithm for product recommendations on its homepage, it would show shoes that were most popular on the site at that time. To personalize those recommendations, it could choose to apply a brand booster. One visitor may see primarily Vans shoes, while another may see shoes from Steve Madden—based on which brands the visitor has shopped across channels. Note that while the original base algorithm would only show any items that are currently popular, applying boosters allows the retailer to show popular items that are also relevant to the individual.

In a similar vein, a B2B site can leverage boosters on its blog to provide relevant article recommendations to each shopper. It could select a "recently published" base algorithm to recommend the newest blog articles to all readers, then apply a category booster to make the recommendations personalized. One visitor might see recommendations for blog posts in the analytics category, while another would see recommendations in project management.

Here's one last example. A visitor researching credit cards on a banking site could be shown offerings that other visitors have looked at with a "co-browse" base algorithm. To make those recommendations more personalized, the algorithm could boost features that are most relevant to the visitor based on his individual preferences, such as co-branded cards or cash-back rewards.

USING BOTH BOOSTERS AND FILTERS

It's worth noting that boosters and filters may seem very similar, because you use them to account for the same variables (such as brand, category, price, etc.), but there are clear differences. Filters allow marketers to have more control over what *types* of items to show, while boosters allow marketers to individualize the *specific* items shown.

Here's an example. Many clothing retailers offer products across different categories (e.g. men, women, kids). One such retailer may choose to apply a category **filter** to recommend only other items on a PDP that are in the same category as the item being viewed. In that case, while viewing a woman's shirt, the shopper would only see recommendations for other women's clothing—not men's or kids' products. Clearly, the filter refines the products being recommended.

In this same example, adding a **booster** can further individualize the women's shirts that are recommended. For example, adding brand and color boosters would leverage the shopper's preferences in these categories, and the site would recommend women's shirts in her favorite brands and colors.

Similarly, a B2B site focused on demand generation could apply a filter to content recommendations on its homepage to only display eBooks, and not any other content type in its library. But the recommendations could be further individualized by applying a booster to highlight a specific eBook that would best fit the individual visitor's stage of the buyer's journey.

Whether you choose to apply filters, boosters, or both is completely dependent on your goals and the needs of your specific visitors. Generally speaking, however, the more you can individualize your recommendations with boosters, the more effective they will be.

VARIATIONS

Finally, you can decide to include some variations in your algorithms. These can take several forms. For example, you can set your homepage recommendations to be randomized (while still being relevant to each individual) so they stay fresh, or you could cap the number of times you show a recommendation to a person to minimize apathy.

Like all of the other aspects of an algorithm that we've described in this chapter, whether or not you include a variation and which variation you choose is completely up to you. It depends on what you think will be most effective for the needs of your particular customers.

CASE STUDY: ZUMIEZ

Zumiez—a multi-channel specialty retailer of apparel, footwear, accessories and gear for skateboarding, snowboarding,

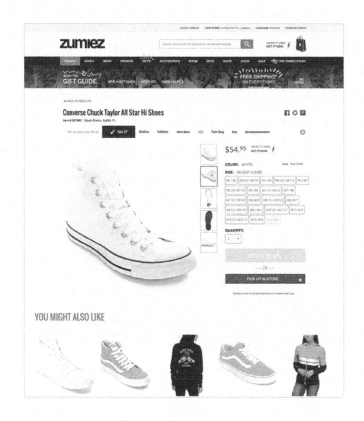

*Zumiez leverages machine-learning algorithms to display individualized
recommendations in the "You Might Also Like" section on this PDP.*

and surf lifestyles—prides itself on its unique customer experience, and has been pushing the envelope to develop personalized experiences for many years. Zumiez shoppers are provided with true one-to-one experiences across the Zumiez site—from the homepage to checkout. Zumiez responds to shoppers' individual preferences to guide which brands they see, which products they discover, and which content they are served.

For example, Zumiez places recommendations in the "Complete the Look," "You Might Also Like" and "Recently Viewed" areas on its product detail pages (PDPs). Zumiez also provides personalized recommendations directly in the search results to help shoppers more quickly discover new products. In both of these cases, a shopper's preferred brands and styles are used to create relevant product recommendations.

Zumiez's efforts have paid off. Shoppers who view and click on a product recommendation on one of the site's PDPs stay on the site nearly four times longer than those who do not click on a recommendation. And shoppers who click a product recommendation convert to a purchase 2.7 times more often than those who do not. These shoppers also spend 2% more per order.

As the case study explains, Zumiez leverages highly individualized recommendations across its site and sees increased engagement, conversions and order value from them. Incorporating all of that data to deliver individualized experiences in real time would be impossible using rules. And while product recommendations date back to the '90s, they were not complex enough to be personalized to every individual. That's how machine learning is changing the game and realizing the one-to-one dream we've been promised for over 20 years.

———————

While we'll get into this in more depth later in the book, it's worth noting now that another big leap forward for one-to-one personalization is the ability to apply this kind of machine-learning personalization not just to products or articles, but to almost anything. Categories, keywords, navigation, promotions, logos, tools, resources, videos, eBooks, brands, calls-to-action, steps in a funnel, etc., can all be algorithmically personalized to show the most relevant, holistic experience to a person based on what he is interested in and who he is.

Today, machine learning is typically being used by forward-thinking marketers and e-commerce professionals. Tomorrow, it will be used ubiquitously by business users across the enterprise.

CHAPTER 2 ENDNOTES

26. computer science. Dictionary.com. Dictionary.com Unabridged. Random House, Inc., http://www.dictionary.com/browse/computer-science?s=t.

27. artificial intelligence. Dictionary.com. Dictionary.com Unabridged. Random House, Inc., http://www.dictionary.com/browse/artificial-intelligence?s=t.

CHAPTER 3

THINK BIGGER, THINK CROSS-CHANNEL

Before you started reading this book, what would come to mind when you thought about personalization? For some marketers, personalization simply means including a name or company field in an email blast. For others, it means Amazon-style recommendations on a website. And for others still, it means presenting people with personalized messages or offers on select channels, such as a website or mobile app. Regardless of what your personalization strategy currently entails, it's worth reviewing the scope of personalization opportunities across a variety of channels.

Cross-channel marketing is a major challenge for marketers in all industries. It isn't enough to master marketing communications through one channel if your current or prospective customers engage with you through many different channels. And for most companies, it's pretty safe to assume that they are. By 2020, there will be four connected devices for every person in the world.[28] By 2025, there will be 5 billion mobile internet users.[29] And Forrester predicts that 58% of total US retail sales will be digitally impacted by 2022 (in other words, some part of the shopping journey for more than half of all retail sales will take place through a digital channel).[30]

Of course, marketers already fundamentally understand the importance of cross-channel marketing. According to a Forrester report, 66% of marketers indicate that cross-channel marketing activities should be integrated.[31] The problem is not that they don't recognize the importance of this kind of marketing: the problem is in the execution. The same report found that only 5% of businesses believe they're truly organized to deliver great cross-channel experiences.[32]

Why the disconnect? We often see that budgets, skill sets and access to technology are spread across companies' IT, marketing and other business groups. It's difficult to create and measure the success of comprehensive campaigns across channels when the skill sets and technologies to do so are decentralized.

There is even misalignment within marketing itself, both organizationally and technologically. Marketers in different disciplines (content marketing, digital marketing, product marketing, marketing operations, etc.) are often using a diverse set of customer analytics tools and other systems. Each of these systems has useful pieces of customer information and insight, but none has the whole picture.

While these challenges make it difficult to execute generic marketing programs across channels, they only become more pronounced with personalization. After all, it's virtually impossible to personalize an experience in a relevant way if you have five different profiles spread across five different systems for a single person. This inability to recognize and speak to a single person across channels is one of the biggest challenges marketers face in cross-channel personalization.

Despite the challenges, in today's multi-channel world, getting cross-channel customer experiences right is worth the effort. In this chapter, we'll highlight the most important channels for personalization and address some of the challenges (and solutions) for executing it effectively across channels.

THE KEY CHANNELS TO PERSONALIZE

Think about the ways in which you interact with companies as a consumer in your own daily life. In most situations, you'll use their websites, either on desktop or mobile. You may also use a mobile app when one is available. You probably receive regular emails from many companies and brands, whether you read them or not. You likely see the company's advertisements on Facebook or other places across the web. You may even receive physical mail from the company. And you probably interact with a human who represents the company or brand from time to time, either in person or on the phone.

When we talk about cross-channel personalization, we mean the ability to provide a consistent and relevant experience across each of these modes of communication using both the rules and machine-learning algorithms described in the previous chapter. Below, we provide details and case studies on each of these channels.

WEBSITE

Many marketers view their website as their most important digital channel—and for good reason. Whether your goal is to drive online sales, generate leads or maximize page views, there are typically some key actions you want visitors to take while on your site (e.g., sign up, download, add to cart, make a purchase, etc.). As a result, many of your online marketing activities are focused on driving traffic to your website and encouraging people to take these steps. Given its importance, the website is often one of the first channels where marketers begin to apply personalization.

Marketers tend to think about personalization taking place in specific spots on a website, such as CTA buttons, product recommendations on product detail pages, or a personalized widget or two on the homepage. As we covered in the last chapter, any area of the site can utilize rules or algorithms to deliver a more relevant experience, from the hero image; to the categories promoted; to the navigation, content and products.

Considering the importance of the website and the central place it holds in many marketers' strategies, it's critical to link the website to other channels to ensure a seamless, cross-channel experience. With all the work that marketers do to drive traffic to their websites, it only makes sense to treat each person to a relevant and engaging experience when they get there. Every page should be a personalized landing page.

CASE STUDY: CARTERA

Cartera Commerce partners with leading airlines that offer loyalty programs, providing a way for airline customers to earn more miles, points or cash by shopping with over 900 retailers they already know and love. The company often sends emails to its regular shoppers containing promotional offers and other information. Cartera wanted a way to remind shoppers of these email offers while they were on the site. But because the offers are not sent to all shoppers, Cartera needed to personalize the site experience to show only the offers that a shopper had already received via email.

By feeding data from its data warehouse into its personalization and customer data platform, Cartera was able to promote consistency between its email and on-site offers. As a result, the company realized a 14% lift in traffic to affiliate stores from lapsed shoppers—a key goal for the company.

WEB APP

For subscription-based industries such as SaaS, financial services, publishing and sometimes retail, the logged-in environment—aka "web application"—is often the primary interface for engaging with end-users and customers. There is enormous opportunity to personalize the logged-in environment, including identifying when users need help and driving them to relevant resources, leveraging features so that they get the most value out of the product, drawing their limited attention to related products and content, and identifying churn risks and upsell opportunities.

CASE STUDY: EIG

Endurance International Group (EIG), a provider of cloud-based platform solutions designed to help small and medium-sized business owners succeed online, leverages in-app personalization to communicate and engage with its customers "in the moment" at different stages of the customers' lifecycle. For instance, while providing web hosting services to customers, EIG saw an upsell opportunity to offer a premium website creation tool to specific audiences. Leveraging in-app personalization to target users with an upsell CTA at the right time, the company saw conversion rates that were four to five times what their traditional promotional email campaigns had produced.

In a related example, EIG's HostGator brand uses in-app personalization to reduce customer support inquiries and costs. EIG identified common technical issues encountered by customers and used personalization to proactively serve up tips and suggestions and the most

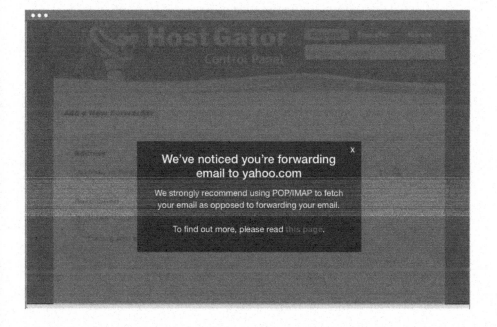

EIG's HostGator brand personalizes its web app experience to provide in-the-moment support to users.

relevant self-help articles. The company estimates that it redirected thousands of support calls and online chats to self-help options in the first six months.

As with all channels, linking the web app to other channels can provide even more relevant experiences. A technology provider can determine a person's area of interest in a product from her behavior on the site during her initial research. It can then leverage that information after she converts and begins to use the product. For example, it can show her an introductory video or in-app tour that highlights features that she might find valuable for that use case. The company can even send her a welcome email with resources relevant to the use case—tying in yet another channel.

MOBILE APP & PUSH NOTIFICATIONS

Mobile apps have become a vital means of engaging and interacting with increasingly untethered audiences. In fact, more than a third of consumers say they expect their mobile apps and websites to be more personalized over the next three years.[33] Yet while marketers are making strides in their website personalization initiatives, mobile is sometimes an afterthought.

Personalization on mobile devices is much like website and web app personalization: it helps users find the most relevant content, categories and products. But personalization is even more critical for mobile experiences. On a desktop website, visitors can hunt for what is relevant to them. While this is not an ideal situation, the larger screen allows visitors to search through large amounts of information to find what they're looking for when there's no choice but to hunt. But the smaller screens of mobile devices make this much more difficult. Marketers need to surface relevant information to mobile users very quickly so users will not give up before finding what they need. This is where targeting different segments and individuals with rules and machine-learning algorithms comes in.

For example, a travel app can share a specific deal only with users who have booked a flight within the past month. Or an e-commerce app can deliver personalized recommendations that boost brand and price affinities to help shoppers find relevant products quickly and easily.

Mobile campaigns are important. But connecting mobile to other channels provides even higher-impact, more relevant experiences.

CASE STUDY: PCH

PCH.com is the web destination for Publishers Clearing House, a multi-channel direct marketer of value-based merchandise, magazines and promotional offers, and a leading provider of digital "play and win" entertainment. It operates multiple websites; when visitors play more games across these sites, PCH can promote more products and display more ads. Visitors, meanwhile, accrue more tokens, earning more opportunities to win prizes.

With no connection between its sites across desktop and mobile, however, visitors had completely different experiences from one to the next. Once visitors completed a game on one site, they were encouraged to visit other PCH sites. But the company couldn't restrict recommendations to the sites that hadn't been visited that day, so visitors were offered games that they had just played. Additionally, PCH could only remind a visitor of abandoned cart items while he was on an e-commerce page. The company wanted to decrease its cart abandonment rate by reminding its visitors about items left in their carts no matter where they were in the PCH universe.

By unifying the experience for each visitor across multiple sites and apps and providing individualized reminder messages, PCH saw a $36,000 increase in revenue the day after implementation and incremental revenue of more than $1 million over a 90-day period.

Push notifications are another important area for personalization in mobile. Push notifications are messages that a company can send a user provided that user has the company's mobile app on his phone or tablet. He does not need to be using the app or even using his phone to be sent a push notification. It simply appears on his device and looks similar to a text message or other mobile alert. As such, push notifications are quite effective for reaching your audience.

But when considering push notifications, don't forget about the close connection people often have with their mobile devices. For many, a mobile phone is the last thing they see before bed and the first thing they see when they awake. One firm estimates that the average person touches her phone a whopping 2,617 times a day![34] The device has become an extension of people's very selves. As such, mobile users want to feel that they can control what appears on their phone, and they will be quick to change settings to avoid any notifications they find obtrusive.

It is critical, therefore, to ensure that any push notification you send is truly relevant and helpful to the individual receiving it. For example, a news app could recognize that a user generally consumes content about politics and entertainment across both the mobile app and desktop site. The app could send the user breaking news stories in only these two categories—and not, for example, in sports. With fewer, more relevant notifications, the user is more likely to find the push notifications a valuable part of his experience with the app, rather than an annoyance.

EMAIL

Email undoubtedly remains a critical communication channel—one used by nearly all businesses today. When thinking about email, it's always important to consider just how many emails your recipients receive each day. The Radicati Group estimates that in 2019, the total number of emails sent and received a day will reach 293 billion. That number is expected to reach 347 billion by the end of 2023.[35] Cutting through that noise is absolutely critical for all businesses, and ensuring that each of your emails is relevant to every individual you reach is a great place to start. You don't want to be tuned out.

Many marketers already leverage personalization in their emails to some degree. In fact, email is the most personalized channel. Yet the majority of those marketers are simply incorporating a recipient's first name or company name, or relying on basic segmentation to personalize their emails.[36] Those tactics are only the start. Let's take some time to explore more advanced ways to personalize an email.

"OPEN-TIME" EMAIL PERSONALIZATION

In order to ensure that the content of your emails is relevant to an individual, you need to consider all you know about that person across channels, particularly in terms of individual behavior, history and preferences. That can be accomplished by leveraging the same rules and algorithms we described in Chapter 2.

But what is relevant to a person at one moment may be obsolete to that same person later. And we all know that you have no control over how and when your email is opened and read. Once the email leaves your servers, the recipient chooses when to consume the information. He or she could open it within a minute, day or week from when it was sent.

During this interval, circumstances can change. A recipient might have already viewed the content you sent, bought the product your email promotes, taken the action your email suggests, or changed his interests altogether. In order to be highly relevant to that recipient, the content of your email should be updated at open time.

How does this work? Ordinarily, when an email is opened, the recipient's email client (such as Microsoft Outlook or Gmail) sends a request to a server to provide any image(s) to display. If you are using open-time email personalization, the personalization platform would make a smart decision about what image(s) to show the moment the message is opened (or re-opened). This decision would be based on everything it knows about the recipient, taking into consideration all of that person's up-to-the-minute behaviors across channels. The personalized content could be product recommendations, promotional offers, eBook or video suggestions, or simply informational messages.

Let's say, for example, that a retailer sends an email containing three product recommendations to a regular customer. Between the time the company sends the email and the moment the customer opens it, the customer has purchased Product 1 via the mobile app, Product 2 went out of stock, and Product 3 dropped in price. When he opens the email, Products 1 and 2 would be substituted with different (but still relevant) recommendations, and Product 3's price would be updated.

Likewise, a web-based application can have an onboarding flow for its new users that contains several emails sent at predetermined times. If the second email in the flow contains a call-to-action to do something in the application that the user has already done, the email can instead suggest that she take another relevant action or recommend appropriate resources to her.

CASE STUDY: INVALUABLE

Invaluable is the world's leading online marketplace for fine art, antiques and collectibles. Fine art and antique collectors are known for their sophisticated and highly individualized tastes. Some seek to build an intimate collection of unique pieces spanning several artists or movements, while others are interested in extremely specific one-of-a-kind pieces. Generic communication will not cut it for these individuals with vastly different tastes.

As part of its personalized email program, Invaluable sends batch emails to customers that contain recommendations tailored to the specific preferences of each person. These recommendations are updated at open time, rather than at send time, to ensure the content is up to date. As a result, one-of-a-kind items that are auctioned and sold rapidly are removed from the emails and replaced with other relevant items. With open-time recommendations, Invaluable has seen a 21% increase in email clickthroughs.

TRIGGERED EMAILS

While open-time email personalization ensures your emails are relevant when recipients are ready to engage with them, triggered emails enable you to proactively send relevant messages at the most opportune moments. Typically, marketers send "batch and blast" emails, which are sent to large lists of recipients at regular times (such as monthly, weekly or even daily). Some marketers, particularly in B2B businesses, send automated "nurture" email sequences to specific groups of opt-in recipients with similar characteristics (e.g., job role, industry, buying stage, etc.). Triggered emails, in contrast, are individual emails sent one at a time when certain criteria are met or shortly thereafter.

Such criteria often include behaviors a person has taken or not taken (like abandoning a cart or not signing into a SaaS application for a certain period of time), catalog updates (such as a product being back in stock or its price reduced), or external conditions (like the weather).

One of the most common use cases for triggered emails in retail is cart abandonment. If a person adds a product to his online shopping cart but leaves the site or app before purchasing, he can receive a triggered email nudging him to complete the purchase. But emails can be triggered even if he doesn't add a product to his cart. If he spends several minutes engaging with a product—reading reviews, scrolling through images, selecting different colors and indicating that he might be willing to purchase—the retailer can immediately send an email asking if he is ready to purchase the product now.

CASE STUDY: CARHARTT

Founded in 1889, Carhartt is a specialty retailer known for its work clothes such as jackets, coats, overalls, coveralls, vests, shirts, jeans, dungarees and fire-resistant clothing. Many of Carhartt's customers buy the same work shirt or boots consistently—they're the same products their parents used, and their grandparents used before them. While each customer identifies with the Carhartt brand and what it stands for, they each have specific needs and preferences.

Carhartt uses its rich understanding of each of its shoppers to deliver relevant experiences across channels. In one example, when a shopper abandons a cart, Carhartt sends him or her a triggered email that contains the item left behind. The company uses this opportunity to show shoppers that it understands their needs by including other relevant products the shopper may like.

These triggered cart abandonment emails combined with personalized recommendations have driven a 7x increase in conversion rate.

Of course, other industries can use triggered emails too. A technology provider could have a page on its site asking visitors to fill out a form to take a free trial or request a demo of the product. If a visitor lands on this page but does not complete the form, the company could send an email triggered by this behavior, asking the person to take the action—perhaps even providing an incentive or an alternate action to drive a conversion.

And that's not all. Insurance companies can send content about how to file storm-damage claims during a big storm. Travel companies can send emails recommending beach vacations during a blizzard. Content publishers can trigger one-off emails to individual subscribers when they have new articles relevant to the recipients' interests. The applications of triggered emails are limitless.

PERSONALIZING THE FREQUENCY AND TIMING OF BULK EMAIL CAMPAIGNS

Triggered emails are useful and highly effective, but they cannot be used in every situation. Sometimes, marketers have a specific message or promotion they want to communicate to a broad audience—either to their whole email list or a portion thereof. Bulk emails, such as weekly promotion emails or monthly newsletters, are valuable in those situations. But to cut down on email clutter, marketers can avoid sending those emails indiscriminately to everyone. They can vary the frequency and timing to match the implicit preferences of each person.

To send better bulk emails, you can pay attention to which

recipients are regularly opening and engaging with your emails, which do so only occasionally, and which never open any emails. Then you can vary the frequency of your emails based on that information. For instance, if you want to send an email newsletter that highlights relevant, recent blog posts for each person on your list, you can do so using open-time personalization. But whether or not a person receives this particular blast will depend on how he has engaged with your emails in the past. A person who has never opened this newsletter may not receive it, while someone who always opens them certainly will.

Beyond the *frequency* of sends, you can also consider the *time of day* that makes the most sense for each individual. Maybe one person is more likely to open emails sent bright and early in the morning, while another tends to open emails during her evening commute.

Essentially, rather than rely on generic best practices of when and how many emails you should send, you can use machine-learning algorithms to learn how each person engages and then the system will pick the most appropriate frequency and timing for that person.

With these different types of email personalization, employed separately or together, you can send much more relevant and timely communications and break through the cacophony.

SEARCH

The search function on any website is incredibly important, as it is a key channel for helping customers find and discover products and content. Visitors who use the search function spell out exactly what they are looking for and, in many cases, are closer to conversion than visitors who don't use search. Yet search is a traditionally underused channel for personalization, and search results are notoriously ineffective for many companies. With all the data that marketers can collect on each of their visitors across channels, this doesn't need to be the case.

To make the most of your on-site search, you should show visitors the most relevant products or content with as little effort (and as few

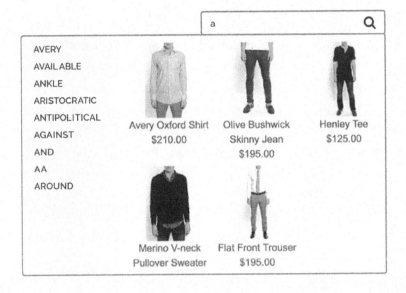

This site shows personalized search results directly into the search bar that are selected and sorted according to a visitor's category preferences.

clicks) as possible. That means that the search results you present should be selected and sorted in a way that is unique to each person, based on the visitor's intent and affinities.

Let's explore an example of a visitor to an e-commerce site who has visited many times. When he begins typing something into the search bar, even if he hasn't completed the words, he can be offered products that he is likely to be interested in based on what the site knows about him so far. If he almost always browses men's clothing, and predominantly men's pants, men's clothing in that category should be sorted toward the top.

Now let's explore a content example. Assume a person landed for the first time on a site for team productivity solutions. She navigates to the resources section of the website and begins to search for a general term related to the space. In the search results, the site should prioritize resources related to her industry (which can be detected automatically—we'll get into more detail next chapter) and her stage of the journey (the beginning). So even though her search is general, the search results can help her find something that is more likely to be relevant to her specific needs.

In short, search results that consider each person's preferences and intent will provide products and content that are relevant to the individual, not to the search term.

DIGITAL ADVERTISING

Digital advertising is a tactic that has long been used by marketers across industries to raise awareness and drive traffic. But take a moment to consider how much ad clutter exists in today's world. The oft-cited number of ads the average person is exposed to daily is 5,000—although there is some debate about the accuracy of that figure.[37] Regardless of the exact number, we can all agree that the average person is exposed to a very large number of ads each day, more than anyone could realistically absorb. And for a marketer, it can be difficult to stand out among all of this clutter, particularly when the intended audience is focused on another task (such as reading content on a publisher's site or scrolling through a social network's newsfeed) when an ad is displayed.

Personalization can help ensure that ads are relevant to each viewer, to better catch each person's attention. Many marketers are already personalizing their digital ads, using both "cold" ads and retargeted ads (ads that are targeted to people who have previously visited a website or used an app). Such retargeted ads will generally contain content relevant to something the visitor looked at while on the site. Yet that content is frequently selected based on limited data, which often means viewers are shown content they are not really interested in (products they have already purchased, eBooks they have already downloaded, etc.).

The key to relevant digital advertising is to leverage all you know about a person from her engagement with your brand across all channels. This will ensure that ads are viewed as valuable, relevant messages rather than spam.

With retargeting, you can advertise to the same segments that you communicate with on your website—or any other segment you create. For example, a B2B site can create segments of visitors in specific industries and then target relevant ads to those industries across the internet. A financial services site could create a segment of visitors who had shown an interest in student loans and then target those visitors with student-related ads. Marketers could even leverage their adtech providers to deliver ads to people who are similar to those in their segments via look-alike models.

CASE STUDY: MAJOR AIRLINE

A major airline wanted to reduce spending on its retargeted

ads without negatively affecting conversions. To accomplish this goal, it sought to target only the people who would be most influenced by the ad to purchase a ticket—not those who were likely to make a purchase anyway.

The company worked to synchronize its first-party customer loyalty data, behavioral data from its website, and third-party media exposure data (the next chapter will provide more detail on these data sources). Once this was done, it could identify loyal customers who had previously abandoned the site—those who were highly likely to convert on their own without reminders from advertising—and exclude this segment from its ads. As a result, the airline significantly reduced media spend while keeping conversions constant.

SOCIAL

According to the Global Web Index, internet users spent an average of 2 hours and 22 minutes on social media in 2018–and that number is even higher for younger audiences.[38] Clearly, it remains an important channel for getting in front of your customers. Some companies have teams of marketers focused on one-to-one responses to complaints or issues, but you can't forget about personalization in social advertising. While the concepts are similar to the advertising section above, it is important enough to deserve its own section.

You can take the data you have available about a person to determine the social ad experience they should receive. For example, you could use predictive scoring (described in the next chapter) to determine which of your shoppers with known email addresses are most likely to purchase jeans in the next few months. Then you can pass those email addresses to Facebook and target those specific individuals (as well look-alikes). You can do the same with any relevant segment to which you'd like to deliver a specific ad via social media.

And, of course, don't forget about feeding ad campaign data back into experiences in other channels. For example, you can keep track of which individuals clicked through to your site from an ad but didn't take an action (make a purchase, download an eBook, request a demo, etc.), and target those people in other ways in other channels going forward.

DIRECT MAIL

Direct mail may sound a little old-fashioned, especially as our world grows increasingly more digital by the day. But marketers across a variety of industries continue to leverage and drive significant value from this tried-and-true channel. As email inboxes become overrun, mail sent to physical inboxes can stand out. Of course, the same concepts of avoiding "batch and blast" generic messages apply to this inbox too.

As with other channels, you want to use the data you've accumulated about your customers and prospects across touchpoints to reach them with effective messaging through the mail. You should aim to:

- Analyze your data to identify segments that are likely to be receptive to direct mail and tailor your message/creative in the mailing to the interests of that segment
- Validate (or acquire) physical mailing addresses for that segment
- Export your lists with up-to-date mailing information to a direct mail service provider for distribution
- Import direct mail campaigns, dates, etc. into your personalization/customer data platform for further reporting, and analysis.

• Target new campaigns and messages to customers/prospects that are included in direct mail campaigns across digital channels

How might companies identify whom to include in direct mail campaigns? A B2B company could mail an invitation for its annual event to known prospects who had engaged meaningfully on its site or spoken with a sales rep in the last six months. An e-commerce company could mail a promotion to shoppers who had made purchases in the past, but not bought anything in the last three months, and were interested in a particular category. Creative marketers can come up with an endless number of ideas, but the key to success with direct mail is data and segmentation (along with a healthy budget).

HUMAN

The human channel is in some ways the most obvious form of personalization: it's very easy to provide a personalized experience to a customer when you're in a one-on-one conversation. At the same time, it's also the least considered form of personalization, as many marketers do not realize that they can use the same principles and data to power their human-based customer interactions as they do their digital interactions. The same valuable information you collect in all of the previously mentioned channels can also be passed on to call center, customer success, and sales personnel to engender more relevant customer engagements.

There are five categories in which humans can be a part of your cross-channel personalization strategy, across both B2C and B2B:

Call Center/Chat Agent: If a person who has been researching credit cards on a website dials the call center for assistance or initiates an online chat session, the support agent should have access to the caller's site behavior when he identifies himself. With access to that data, the agent can see what the caller's preferences are and what he has been researching to provide the most relevant assistance possible. The agent can either provide the assistance on her own, or use machine learning-driven suggestions from the system.

In-Store Associate: If a shopper has been researching mobile phones and accessories on a wireless carrier's website, but later enters the physical store, the in-store associate holding a clienteling application could look up the customer based on an email or loyalty ID and receive relevant promotions, offers and recommendations to discuss with the client.

In-Branch Associate: When a customer enters a bank and provides his account information to the teller, she can access his complete customer profile. She could note if he has been researching any products or exhibiting any churn warning signs—so she can guide the conversation toward upselling or troubleshooting as appropriate.

Sales Team: A B2B salesperson prospecting into an account can provide a personalized experience too. When preparing for a sales call, she can look into the activity of all visitors associated with the account—including an account's activity history, preferred solutions, categories and content—to steer the conversation in a relevant direction even before asking discovery questions.

Customer Success/Support Team: Once an account becomes a customer, the support or customer success team can provide a personalized experience based on in-app behavior as well. The team can stay on top of how often users in the account log in, what features they use, and how engaged they tend to be. Instead of reaching out to ask how a customer is doing and if he's satisfied with the product, the team can reach out with specific actions and ideas for how a customer can get more value for the solution (not to mention identify potential churn risks early!)

As you might have noticed from these examples, the trick to tying the online and offline component is having the right data, which we'll explore further in the next chapter.

CROSS-CHANNEL MATURITY CURVE

What we have explained so far can seem overwhelming to some marketers, particularly those who are not using personalization at all or only using it in a single channel. As we explained earlier in this chapter, cross-channel marketing of any kind is difficult. Most marketers we speak to are not as advanced as they would like to be in their cross-channel personalization efforts. Typically, most strategies we've seen fall roughly at one of these stages: beginner, intermediate and advanced.

Beginner: Marketers at this stage are typically only personalizing one digital channel (such as web, mobile app, email, ads or search). They have only one team involved in their personalization efforts, and their main challenges involve getting started, defining a strategy and working out a repeatable process.

Intermediate A: The intermediate stage has two different paths. In the first path, marketers have progressed to personalize two or three digital channels. Their main challenge stems from the difficulties that arise from coordinating across multiple internal teams (we will cover some of these challenges in Chapter 7).

Intermediate B: In the second intermediate path, marketers are personalizing in only one digital channel (as in the beginner stage),

	Beginner	Intermediate Option A	Intermediate Option B	Advanced
Channels	1 digital channel	2 or 3 digital channels	Sync with other systems	Agent interactions + multiple channels
	Web Mobile App Email Search Digital Ads	Web Mobile App Email Search Digital Ads	CRM Marketing Automation Data Warehouse Etc.	Call Center/Chat In-Store Customer Success Sales Representative
Benefit	Only 1 team	Cross-Channel	Better data for more relevant experiences	Full cross-channel
Challenge	Getting started	Cross-team coordination needed	Data integration if not available out-of-the-box	Additional integration

The Cross-Channel Personalization Maturity Curve

but they are syncing data from multiple systems to deliver better targeted experiences. They typically face challenges around data coordination.

Advanced: Advanced cross-channel personalization strategies incorporate the human element—whether in a call center, in a store, or from sales/customer success professionals (as described earlier). Technology integrations tend to be the main challenge at this stage.

Clearly, most marketers do not go straight from static, unconnected digital channels right to advanced cross-channel personalization. Rather, cross-channel personalization is an ongoing process of learning, testing and coordinating..

No matter where you fall in the maturity curve, in order to implement a personalization strategy across channels, you need four main components:

1. The ability to track behavior across channels

2. The ability to unite data from multiple channels and systems across the organization (CRM, marketing automation, data warehouse, etc.) in one central location, such as a customer data platform or "CDP"

3. The ability to stitch this data together to establish a single profile for each individual

4. The ability to leverage all of your data to deliver personalized experiences in each channel in real time at the one-to-one level

Accomplishing all of these aims is completely doable, and it all starts with data.

CHAPTER 3 ENDNOTES

28. Karla Lant, "By 2020, There Will Be 4 Devices for Every Human on Earth," futurism.com, Jun 2017, https://futurism.com/by-2020-there-will-be-4-devices-for-every-human-on-earth.

29. GSM Association, "The Mobile Economy 2018," https://www.gsma.com/mobileeconomy/wp-content/uploads/2018/05/The-Mobile-Economy-2018.pdf.

30. Forrester Research, "Forrester Data: Digital-Influenced Retail Sales Forecast, 2017 To 2022 (US)," Nov 2017, https://www.forrester.com/report/Forrester+Data+DigitalInfluenced+Retail+Sales+Forecast+2017+To+2022+US/-/E-RES140811?objectid=RES140811.

31. Forrester Research, "The Omnichannel Commerce Playbook for 2016," 2016, https://www.forrester.com/The+Omnichannel+Commerce+Playbook+For+2017/-/E-PLA850.

32. Ibid.

33. Sitecore, "How to Keep Pace with Consumer Expectations," conducted by Vanson Bourne, May 2016, http://www.sitecore.net/en/resources/index/white-papers/mobile-research-whitepaper.

34. Julia Naftulin, "Here's how many times we touch our phones every day," Business Insider, Jul 2016, http://www.businessinsider.com/dscout-research-people-touch-cell-phones-2617-times-a-day-2016-7.

35. The Radicati Group, "Email Statistics Report, 2019-2023," Feb 2019, https://www.radicati.com/wp/wp-content/uploads/2018/12/Email-Statistics-Report-2019-2023-Executive-Summary.pdf.

36. Evergage Inc. and Researchscape International, "2019 Trends in Personalization," Apr 2019, http://www.evergage.com/resources/ebooks/trends-in-personalization-survey-report/.

37. J. Walker Smith, "The Myth of 5,000 Ads," Hill Holiday, http://cbi.hhcc.com/writing/the-myth-of-5000-ads/.

38. Saima Salim, "How much time do you spend on social media? Research says 142 minutes per day," Digital Information World, Jan 2019, https://www.digitalinformationworld.com/2019/01/how-much-time-do-people-spend-social-media-infographic.html.

CHAPTER 4

GARBAGE IN, GARBAGE OUT

We've all heard the expression: "Garbage in, garbage out," which means that the quality of the input to a process will determine the quality of the output. If your inputs are bad, then your output will be too. The adage applies to any type of personalization, but especially to one-to-one personalization. Even the most advanced machine-learning algorithm designed to provide a highly individualized experience won't be successful without a deep understanding of each individual, and that understanding comes from the data.

Think about it this way: if you're a sales associate in a retail store, you probably want to provide a personalized experience to every customer. But if you're trying to help a shopper find what she's looking for or to recommend additional products she may be interested in, your help will be completely ineffective if you don't know anything about her. You need to have a conversation with her before you can offer any valuable assistance. Likewise, you will not be an effective store associate if you don't know anything about your store's products and inventory. In the digital world, the data you collect acts as that conversation, as well as your inventory knowledge, to help you form an accurate representation of each person and your business.

In the context of personalization, "bad data" can have several different meanings. Data is bad or ineffective when it's incorrect, when it becomes outdated, when it's inadequate, and/or when it's siloed.

Incorrect Data: It's easy to understand why using incorrect data would lead to inappropriate or inaccurate personalized experiences: if an input is wrong, the output will be wrong too. For example, you could use data from your CRM to deliver an email to customers who are using your product for a particular use case. But if that data was entered incorrectly into your CRM for certain customers, the resulting email will be targeted incorrectly and won't make sense.

Outdated Data: Just because something was true a day or even a minute ago doesn't mean that it's still true. Technology allows us to move very quickly, and personalization that doesn't keep up won't be accurate. For example, if a visitor to a travel site researches and books a ski vacation all in one session, it won't make sense to recommend additional ski vacation packages to him via an email or when he's on the site again later that day (although it may still make sense to recommend ski-related content to him). While it is true that those packages *were* relevant to him recently, they are not *still* relevant to him.

Inadequate Data: Although it might not be obvious to the topic of "bad data," not having enough data can produce less-than-accurate personalized experiences too. We found in our annual study that one of the most common criteria marketers use to target personalization campaigns is pages viewed.[39] This is a good start, but understanding that a person clicked on a few specific pages doesn't tell the whole story. Was she interested in what she found on those pages, or not interested at all? If it's a retail site, is she a loyalty program member? What are her favorite categories and brands? If it's a B2B site, at which stage of the journey is she? What topics is she interested in? If it's a financial services site, is she an existing customer? What products does she use? If you only have a few data points to paint a portrait of your visitor, you'll only create a hasty sketch.

Siloed Data: Most marketers collect and store data on one individual in multiple places; in fact, Forrester found that marketers have customer data stored across 15 different places, on average.[40] This data can be found across CRM applications, loyalty systems, marketing automation platforms, analytics tools, data warehouses and other areas. Sometimes the challenge is that a company's data is inadequate—specifically when it comes to behavioral data, as we'll see later in the chapter. But more often, the company has plenty of data to use for personalization, but the data isn't easily accessible through the silos. The ability to bring data together into a single location is a critical first step to one-to-one personalization.

Clearly, if you have one or more of these issues with your data, your personalized experiences will be affected. And realistically, a personalized experience based on incorrect data isn't truly personalized at all. It's an endeavor that misses the mark.

DATA TYPES

Throughout the book, we have described experiences and scenarios where data was collected and acted on to personalize an experience. But what specific data types are useful for personalization? Any data that gives a marketer insight into an individual can be used. That data typically falls into one of four buckets: attribute data, first-party behavioral data, survey data and third-party data.

ATTRIBUTES

Attributes describe any characteristic of a visitor. They can be derived from two key sources:

Web Attributes: These attributes are detected as soon as a person lands on a site. They are particularly valuable in helping you personalize an experience for first-time visitors who have not yet interacted with your site, although they can be used in many other situations as well. Some common web attributes include:

- Geolocation
- Source (such as search, email, social, paid ad, referring site, etc.)
- Industry
- Company
- Company size (revenue or employee count)
- Technology stack
- Time of day
- Browser type
- Device type

CASE STUDY: CONSUMER FINANCIAL SERVICES COMPANY

A premier consumer financial services company is a leading provider of private label credit cards in the US. Through its vast network of partners, the company offers a wide range of credit products for financing the purchase of various consumer goods and services. The company uses its homepage to promote offers from its retail partners from across the country. Real estate on the homepage is limited, so the company was unable to promote any regional offers—opting instead to focus on national retailers that were more broadly applicable to its visitors.

By targeting the site's promotions by geolocation, the company was able to build a single campaign with multiple experiences that delivered targeted offers to visitors within the available website space. With this campaign, a visitor from California would see deals specific to that region, while a visitor from New York would see different, relevant offers. The effort drove a 200% increase in total clickthroughs from the offers on the company's homepage.

Database Attributes: Rather than being detected from the web automatically, database attributes are pulled from a database-driven system such as a CRM or a data warehouse. They can include anything that you store in those systems, such as whether the visitor is a prospect or customer—and what type of customer he is (e.g., a high-value customer, a customer in a particular category, etc.). In order to tie a website visitor to his data in another system, you need some kind of identifier (such as an email address) for that visitor. Some examples of database-driven systems that can be used for personalization:

- *Customer Relationship Management (CRM) Systems,* such as Salesforce, Netsuite or Microsoft Dynamics
- *Email and Marketing Automation Platforms,* such as Oracle Eloqua or ExactTarget (Salesforce Marketing Cloud)
- *Analytics,* such as Google Analytics or Adobe Analytics
- *E-Commerce Platforms,* such as Magento or SAP Hybris
- *Content Management Systems (CMS),* such as Wordpress or Adobe Experience Manager
- *Tag Managers,* such as IBM Digital Data Exchange or Tealium
- Other systems such as *Data Management Platforms (DMPs), Point of Service (POS) Systems, Enterprise Resource Planning (ERP) systems, data warehouses, call center solutions* and more

CASE STUDY: SQUAW VALLEY ALPINE
MEADOWS

Squaw Valley Alpine Meadows (SVAM), an internationally renowned mountain resort, caters to a wide swath of customers—from season pass holders to first-time skiers, tour groups to families. Each of its visitors has unique interests and priorities. SVAM determined that there were eight key personas it needed to target on its site, each requiring a different voice and unique content. The company needed a way to personalize the website experience to these specific segments to drive increased engagement and conversion.

One group it wanted to target was its high-value season pass holders. Season pass holders cannot be detected automatically from the web, but that data did exist in the company's CRM system. By bringing its CRM data into its personalization and CDP engine, SVAM was able to target a homepage experience specifically to season pass holders with messaging that appealed uniquely to them. These personalized experiences increased conversions and revenue per user among several key segments.

FIRST-PARTY BEHAVIORAL DATA

First-party behavior refers to any action taken on your website, in your app or in response to your push notifications or email campaigns. It can be broken down into four major categories:

Site-Wide (and App-Wide) Behavior: Site-wide behavior encompasses general behavioral analytics such as:

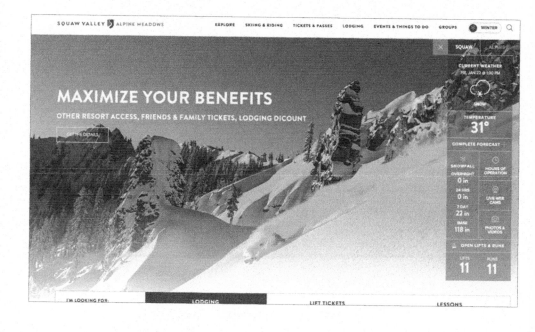

SVAM has several homepage experiences, including this one for season pass holders (leveraging attribute data from its CRM system).

- Total number of site visits
- Total number of logins
- Total number of pages or screens viewed
- Total time spent on-site or in-app
- Average time spent per page
- Time elapsed since last site visit
- Total number of articles read, purchases made, videos viewed, etc.

This information can be useful in a number of ways. Notably, you can apply it to target messages, notifications or experiences to first-time visitors or users. Here, the number of times a person has visited the site or app is important in determining the experience he receives. You can also use site- and app- wide behavior to target a campaign to returning visitors who have not engaged with the channel in a defined period of time.

Page Visit Behavior: Page visit behavior refers to data about specific page or screen views for an individual, such as:
- Specific pages or screens viewed
- Number of times each page/screen was viewed

While site-wide and app-wide behavior refers to such metrics as the *total* number of pages or screens viewed—or the average amount of time spent per page—page visit behavior refers to the *specific* pages visited or screens viewed. For example, page visit behavior would tell you that a person viewed Product Page A three times and Product Page B once. While still a bit high-level, this data can be valuable nevertheless.

Deep Behavior and Context: Deep behavior goes a step further than the previous categories and involves information about the page viewed as well as specific behaviors taken or not taken on that page.

The information includes:
- Time spent on a page
- Mouse movement
- Scrolling
- Hovering
- Inactivity
- In-page context (category, tags, brand, color, keywords, etc.)

Deep behavior and context combines the level of engagement for each page with the attributes of the page itself to provide an accurate indication of an individual's affinities, interests and intent. This type of information is critical to true one-to-one personalization.

Campaign Engagement: Campaign engagement refers to the actions an individual has taken in response to any of your campaigns across channels. It includes behaviors such as:
- Personalized experience views and clickthroughs
- Email opens and/or clicks
- Push notification dismissals or clickthroughs
- Correlation of the above to device, time of day, or other variables

Derivative in nature, this data is immensely valuable, as it builds your understanding of each visitor and further informs your one-to-one personalization efforts.

Let's explore how these four behavioral data types differ with an example. Let's say a customer visits a retail site. He's a regular shopper and has viewed several product pages over the past month.

If you (as a marketer looking to personalize his experience) had access only to his *site-wide behavior*, you would only know that he has visited the site three times over the last month and that his last visit was one week ago. You would know that he typically spends an average of five minutes on the site and that he has viewed 20 pages on the site overall. With this information, you don't know anything about his individual preferences or his intent for this site visit, but you could include him in a segment for loyal shoppers, for example.

If you had access to *page visit behavior* as well, you would know which of the 20 pages he has viewed. You would understand that he has clicked on five product pages within the shirt category, five product pages within the pants category, and six product pages within the shoe category. These products are evenly spread across three different brands and five different colors. From that information, you might conclude that he had no brand or color preference, and that he is slightly more interested in shoes than shirts or pants. You could provide him with product recommendations with a simple co-browse algorithm to show him products that other shoppers viewed, but you wouldn't be able to truly individualize those recommendations to him.

But if you had access to *deep behavioral data*, you could understand much more. You would know that while he viewed the category of shoes slightly more than shirts or pants, he spent three times as long viewing shirts than either of the other categories. You would know that when he clicked on Brand A, he immediately clicked away. You would know that he showed much more engagement while looking at shirts in blue and green than he did with any of the other colors. And you would know that he has spent several minutes engaging with a product page for a particular blue shirt, scrolling through photos and reviews, even going so far as selecting a size—without yet adding the item to his cart.

Now, if you applied a machine-learning algorithm that delivered personalized recommendations based not only on popularity but also on each shopper's preferred categories and colors, the shopper in this example would see top-selling blue and green shirts. Given the alignment of these items with his affinities, you would dramatically increase your chances of engaging him and driving clickthroughs. Taking this a step further, if he does click through on certain shirts, adds one or two to his cart, or makes a purchase, your *campaign engagement* data would automatically inform the personalization platform of this action. It could then, for example, remind him of items left in his cart and avoid suggesting items he already purchased when he visits the site again.

If you want to deliver true one-to-one experiences with the sophisticated algorithms we described in Chapter 2, you need deep behavioral data and contextual data combined with campaign engagement data to maximize relevancy. That is not to say that the other data types are worthless: we have shown numerous examples of successful campaigns that leverage all data types. But as we have seen, one-to-one communication powered by machine learning is the direction the world is headed, and deep behavioral and campaign engagement data is driving much of this transformation.

SURVEY DATA

While you can learn a lot about an individual from all the data types that have already been described, sometimes the best way to learn something about a person is simply to ask. Most of us don't enjoy taking surveys, so this may not sound like a good option. But the surveys we tend to dislike are those that are lengthy, tedious and don't seem to provide any value to our lives.

If there is something specific you want to know about your customers to help you provide a better experience, go ahead and ask them—but keep it brief. A short question or two can color in the picture you've created with the rest of your data and will likely be more useful to your personalization efforts than a lengthy survey. Think about what you are trying to learn about your customers or visitors and how you would treat each of them differently based on what you learn. Here are some things to consider when formulating your survey questions:

- What questions will customers not mind answering, because they're quick and not overly personal?
- What would each response tell us about the person?
- How would we use the answers to deliver an experience that provides value to the customer?

Once you have your question or questions ready, you can display a short survey on your site or in your app, either to everyone who visits or only to those who have taken a specific action, spent a specific amount of time on the site, or fallen into some other relevant segment. Use their answers to deliver appropriate, personalized experiences, either in the moment and/or at some point in the future. When you take action on the information you receive right away, visitors will understand why you asked the question and appreciate the immediate value received in exchange for their feedback.

For example, a fashion retailer could deploy a quick and visually interesting survey on its site in order to better understand its shoppers. Visitors would be shown a few images of activities—such as yoga, hiking, DIY crafts, etc.—and be asked which they enjoy doing in their free time. Then, once they answer, they could be shown product recommendations or helpful articles relevant to that particular persona. The retailer also now has that information about each shopper's interests for use in future campaigns.

THIRD-PARTY DATA

Finally, data from third parties can be leveraged for personalization as well. Any action an individual takes across the broader internet— from searches conducted on search engines, to surveys taken on media sites, to pages viewed and forms submitted—can be used, as can any additional attribute data collected by outside sources. This data is often aggregated by a variety of vendors and sold for targeting and analytics purposes. Such vendors include data management platforms (DMPs), which focus on the B2C market; ABM analytics providers, which focus on the B2B market; and social media sites. Some common examples of third-party data used in personalization are:

- Demographic data (e.g., age, urban/suburban, income level, etc.)
- Firmographic data (e.g., industry, average selling price, budget cycle, etc.)
- Buying signals (e.g., in the market for a new car/home/technology solution, etc.)
- Self-defined attributes (e.g., relationship status on Facebook, career data on LinkedIn, etc.)

PREFERENCES AND INTENT

Marketers sometimes wonder how such a surplus of detailed data can possibly be harnessed and effectively used. The key is to turn everything you learn about an individual into something you can act on. But before you can do that, you need machine learning to interpret the data and use it to determine people's preferences (or affinities) and intent.

Affinity modeling with machine learning can synthesize immense amounts of data to tell a clear story about an individual that evolves over time. This is yet another way that machine learning is changing the game in one-to-one communication. To illustrate, let's refer back to what we know about the retail shopper in the previous example.

Affinity modeling can take all of that deep data you collected about your shopper and tell you clearly that shirts are his favorite category, that he does not like Brand A, and that his favorite colors are blue and green—so that you don't have to manually dive into the data and uncover these insights yourself. As our example illustrated, with this information your algorithms can boost the shopper's preferences in his product recommendations and other experiences across the site.

The same process applies to more than just retail examples, of course. With affinity modeling, a technology provider could uncover a prospect's preferred use case, content categories, content types, keywords, authors and more to boost those affinities in content recommendations across the site. Or in the financial services sector, a company could uncover the specific features a prospective customer is seeking in a credit card or an insurance plan, for example, and highlight those offerings.

Understanding a visitor's preferences isn't where it ends, however. Once you understand a person's preferences, you also need to identify his intent in the moment so that you can understand what he is browsing for and trying to accomplish right now. The key to understanding intent is real-time data. Without it, you will always be responding to an individual's intent the *next time* he is on the site.

An example might help underscore the importance of real-time data. Let's say you walk into a big-box store to look at storage solutions. You ask a sales associate for a recommendation, and he suggests an action figure. You tell him that his suggestion doesn't make any sense; you're interested in storage, not children's toys. He reminds you that you were interested in children's toys the last time you visited, and therefore that is what he has for you. But if you come back in a few hours, he says, he can recommend a storage solution; it will take a little while to update your intent in their system.

Although the above example sounds outlandish, it is exactly the type of experience you will give site visitors if you can't respond to intent in real time. But what does it look like when you do have access to real-time data? Returning to the previous example—the retail shopper—the data shows that the shopper is demonstrating intent to purchase a blue shirt. With that information available to you in real time, you could launch a campaign to encourage him to purchase that shirt right now, whether by reminding him of any existing offers or credits available, or, perhaps, by letting him know about your free returns policy.

Here are a few other examples. If a B2B site can uncover precisely why someone is on the site— doing some general research on a certain technology versus drilling down into specific products—and show him relevant information, he is more likely to react favorably than if he were blasted with promotions. Or, if a bike shopper on a B2C site is trying to decide between road bikes and mountain bikes, he will have a much more positive experience if the site delivers content that helps him understand the bikes' different styles and uses than if it pushes products at him. Only once it's clear that he's going down a particular path, the site should help him understand the specific features and benefits of a particular type or model of bike.

Preferences and intent are incredibly nuanced. Getting it right can mean the difference between featuring a product that is high-end versus one that's mid-range, or recommending a case study versus a blog post. And the visitor may not even notice that an experience is tailored to him. In a world where marketers are competing for consumers' digital attention, showing people something relevant and timely can keep them exploring your site longer and can drive them to convert sooner.

PREDICTIVE MODELING

Identifying preferences and intent using affinity modeling allows you uncover a person's *current state* (or past state, if you're not operating in real time). But what about the future state? For that, you need predictive modeling.

With predictive modeling, you leverage machine learning to predict a future event based on an understanding of past events. When a predictive model has access to mass volumes of data inputs, including the real outcomes of situations similar to the ones you're hoping to predict, it will identify patterns and predict what will happen when it is given new inputs.

For example, if you wanted to predict which of your SaaS customers are likely to churn, you need to give your model an understanding of which customers have churned in the past, as well as all of the data you have available on those customers (such their firmographic or demographic details, their plan level, their login behavior and how they interacted with your application, how they engaged with your emails over time, and much more). The model can take in all of this information to identify patterns in churned customers vs. retained customers. Then, you can feed it data on all of your existing customers so that it can predict which current customers are most likely to churn.

You can predict just about anything you think would be valuable for your business, provided you have enough relevant data to train the model. Some of the main predictions that businesses may find helpful may include a person's:

- Likelihood to purchase
- Likelihood to request a demo or complete an application
- Likelihood to churn (in a subscription-based business)
- Likelihood to purchase again (in a retail business)
- Likelihood to open or click through from an email
- Likelihood to unsubscribe from an email list
- Value to your business within a certain timeframe
- Total predicted lifetime value
- Predicted response to any given promotion or campaign

- Likelihood to qualify for any of your segments (as described in Chapter 2—such as a loyal shopper segment)

Some of these have a lot of value when predicted in real time. For example, if you want to know which promotion will appeal to each individual website visitor, you can use a model to predict how each person will respond to each promotion—and then display that promotion in real time (we'll dive more into this type of personalization in Chapter 6). Or, if you want to know if you should offer a small discount to encourage an engaged shopper to convert, you can use a model to predict whether he is likely to convert in this visit. If there is a high likelihood he will convert, you don't need to lose revenue from a discount (as he is to likely buy without one).

Other predictions are less important to act on in real time, but can make a big impact on your business. When you can predict which of your customers are likely to churn, you can run marketing campaigns designed to incentivize them to stay or work to resolve any issues immediately. When you can predict which of your past retail shoppers are unlikely to return and purchase again, you can send more targeted emails to them to encourage them to come back.

The applications of predictive modeling are endless, yet it's important to note that these models can only be effective if they have access to a lot of accurate data. When we say "a lot" of data, we mean data from many different individuals (breadth), as well as many different data points for each individual (depth). Without a breadth of data, the model will not have enough situations to learn from. And without a depth of data, the model will be missing big sections of the picture. For example, if you want to predict an individual's lifetime value—but you're only training your predictive models with website data—the prediction will understandably be less accurate than it would be if you trained the models with data from in-store, mobile, call centers, emails, etc. In another example, if the model doesn't know that a customer has just called your company with a complaint, it will be missing a key churn indicator.

In other words, predictive models can be most accurate when they have access to a well-populated customer data platform.

CENTRALIZED DATA AND CUSTOMER DATA PLATFORMS

We can't end a chapter on data without talking about where you need to store all this data. As we mentioned earlier, most businesses store customer data in multiple locations across their organizations. But delivering relevant, one-to-one experiences requires access to and interpretation of all of that customer data—no matter where it currently lives.

The customer data platform (CDP) has emerged as the solution to this siloed data problem. Other tools, like the CRM, were historically thought to be the single central location for customer data. But most of those solutions were built in a different era when database structures were simpler and volumes of data lower. Most importantly, they were not built to handle the mass volumes of behavioral data we can access today.

Think back to our discussion of behavioral data earlier in this chapter. When you collect in-depth behavioral website data such as time spent on each page, time spent hovering and scrolling on each page, inactive time on each page, etc., it quickly adds up. And when you combine those site behaviors with mobile behavioral data, email or push notification campaign engagement, in-person interactions from a store or branch location, call center or online chat data, and any attribute data from any other system—you have way more data than a typical CRM can handle, in formats a CRM is not equipped to process.

And, of course, we know that none of this data means anything unless it can be interpreted and analyzed. Knowing that someone visited a website on a certain date and spent three minutes browsing across 11 pages doesn't mean much unless you can put it in context and, through affinity and predictive modeling, infer his preferences and predict his future actions. CRMs were certainly not built for that.

The CDP category is still being defined, so no two CDPs offer the exact same set of features. But all CDPs must offer, at their core, a single unified customer profile.

IDENTITY RESOLUTION WITHIN THE UNIFIED CUSTOMER PROFILE

Central to any CDP is a unified customer profile. Each person, whether known or anonymous, must have a single profile that contains all data relevant to him or her from a variety of sources.

This profile should include as much data as possible to help understand the person including purchases, browsing history, email interactions, attributes, subscriptions, loyalty membership and status, interests and preferences, browser type, location, demographics, predictive scores and more. And this profile should include and unify many identifying data elements such as cookies, email address, full name, physical address, phone number, system ID, etc. Once the profile is in place, it can be used as the foundation of any personalization campaign across any channel going forward.

While the goal is to create a single profile for each individual, it's still possible to end up with multiple profiles for the same person. Thus, when data comes from different sources, it needs to be stitched together into one single profile. This is simple when there is clear identifying information (for instance, the same email address), but not every person will clearly identify themselves in every channel for every interaction. Consider these situations:

1. A visitor to a B2B site fills out a form to download a report and includes her name and email address. Now the company can identify her when she is on the website. However, some time later she uses a different browser. Her named profile still exists, but after that point, a new profile is created to capture her website activity as an anonymous visitor.

2. A shopper in a retail store makes several purchases with his loyalty number. The retailer has his name and other identifying information through the loyalty program, as well as a history of his in-store purchases. Later, he browses the e-commerce site numerous times but never makes a purchase or identifies himself in any way, so his named in-store profile remains separate from his anonymous website behavioral profile.

3. A customer of a bank or insurance company receives an email from that firm, reads the email, and then clicks through to the website. Later she calls the call center to discuss the same topic covered in the email and that she researched on the company's website. In this scenario, she may be seen as three different people across the company's email, web and call center systems.

The separate profiles created in these situations all contain useful customer data, but each one doesn't fully account for the person's true and complete identity. CDPs need to be able to stitch profiles together when the data becomes available to do so.

For instance, let's assume that Mary Smith has a profile in a company's CDP that encompasses data from several different channels (store, call center, mobile app, etc.). But Mary has never identified herself on her laptop. Therefore, she has one "Mary Smith" profile and one "anonymous" profile in the CDP. The CDP needs to be able to merge both of these profiles together once she identifies herself in some way—such as clicking through from an email to the company's site while on her laptop. Once it becomes clear that the anonymous person is actually Mary Smith, both profiles need to be stitched together to create a full picture of Mary.

The same is true across any profile in the CDP. The CDP needs to constantly monitor identifying information to determine if two or more profiles represent the same identity. This can be done through deterministic matching or probabilistic (heuristic) matching.

With deterministic matching, the CDP stitches profiles together based on clear, unique identifiers such as system ID or email address. Here's an example for a site focused on demand generation. Let's say an unidentified prospect views a technology provider's website twice on his laptop and once on his mobile phone without providing his email or filling out a form. The tech provider would create two profiles for this person: one (Profile ABC) containing his laptop behavior, and one (Profile XYZ) containing his mobile behavior.

The next time the prospect returns to the site, this time on his laptop, he downloads a white paper—providing his email address in the process. The tech provider would now be able to update Profile ABC to contain the prospect's name and email address, as well as a history of all the actions the prospect has taken on his laptop so far. But Profile XYZ—the mobile profile—is still anonymous. Later, he clicks through on an email from the tech provider to the site while on his mobile device. The tech provider should now be able to merge Profile XYZ (containing behavior from the mobile device) with Profile ABC (containing laptop behaviors), as it can identify that those profiles are the same person. Now, when a salesperson reaches out to this prospect, she will have a complete profile that includes his mobile, laptop and email behaviors. And any personalization that takes place across those channels can be fueled from the same profile.

Anonymous user profile with deep
customer data

Mary Smith is identified in one of many
potential ways

Mary's anonymous profile is merged with her
known identity to create one robust profile

*With deterministic profile matching, the CDP stitches profiles together
based on clear, unique identifiers.*

But matching isn't a perfect science. Oftentimes, a CDP needs to use "fuzzy" logic, called probabilistic or heuristic matching. In these situations, there is no clear identifier. Instead, the CDP makes an educated guess about profiles that likely represent the same individual based on a combination of different data such as location, behavior, etc.

One final note about identity. It's certainly not ideal to have several profiles that reflect one individual, but it's just as bad (if not worse) to have data from more than one person reflected in a single profile. In other words, it is essential that a CDP doesn't *incorrectly merge profiles together.*

Each business has a different set of identity sources and a different tolerance for error and false positives. It's important to be able to add your own rules to instruct the CDP of your view of the trustworthiness of different data types and decide what action to take when there is a conflict. This is very business-specific, so a business should have control in this area.

For example, you may want to ensure your CDP merges profiles if they match on one type of field, such as email address, but not on another, such as physical address. Other businesses may want to match on email address *and* physical address, but prioritize email over physical address. You may also want to value some sources more highly than others if two sources conflict. For example, the email address from which a person clicks through to the website may be more likely to be accurate than the email he adds to a website form (where he may add a fake email address to try to download a piece of content, for example). Or, for example, you may regard a customer's loyalty ID as more trustworthy than the phone number.

There are different scenarios that each business should explore to determine what logic makes sense to apply. Resolving identities correctly is critical to successful personalization, so it's worth it to put in some work upfront to ensure the CDP takes the correct actions when merging and stitching profiles.

ACTING ON CDP DATA

The act of bringing data from across an organization into a central location, such as a CDP, isn't something that a reasonable person would undertake just for fun. There must always be an end goal dictating how this data will be put to use. Most often, that goal is either analysis, activation or both.

ANALYSIS: COMBINING A CDP WITH BUSINESS INTELLIGENCE

Let's start with analysis. Businesses often have a lot of questions about how their business is doing and what it could be doing better. The challenge is not that the data doesn't exist to answer these questions, it's that the data is scattered across the organization.

But once you have all of your data from many different sources together in a CDP, there's a lot you can learn. You can answer nearly any question you can conceive, such as:

- Which customers or groups of customers are most profitable to my business?
- What do my profitable customers have in common? How are they typically acquired? Do they share similar demographics (for B2C) or firmographics (for B2B)? What are their interests?
- How well do my marketing programs perform? Which marketing tactics appeal to which types of customers?
- Which products most appeal to different customer segments? Do I have the right inventory mix to address demand?

Most CDPs will offer the ability to do basic analysis on their own, but giving a business intelligence (BI) solution access to CDP data can answer these types of advanced questions that business analysts typically ponder.

ACTIVATION: USING CDP DATA TO PERSONALIZE

The ability to transform your customer data into critical business insights is a key benefit of the CDP. Ultimately, however, you don't bring data together just to learn something. Most companies want to do something with what they have learned. That's where activation comes in.

Activation on CDP data can take many forms. For example, you can act on CDP data to:

- Determine which promotions or offers to target to each person based on his or her past behaviors, interests, loyalty program status, etc.
- Deliver digital ads only to people most likely to be affected by them—and avoid spending money advertising to loyal customers who are more likely to purchase on their own
- Talk to target ABM accounts or open sales opportunities in a specific and targeted way across channels
- Ensure website and email CTAs are always relevant to the recipient (for example, removing/changing CTAs for actions a person has already taken)
- Recommend content, products, brands, and more based on everything that is known about that person in the moment while they're on your site or reading your emails

Essentially, activation of CDP data looks like all the different forms of cross-channel personalization we described in the last chapter.

There are two main ways to activate on CDP data: the CDP can push data to other systems to use, or it can take action directly—that is, if it also offers personalization functionality.

Pushing data to other systems is essential CDP functionality because no single martech solution can exist in isolation—and no single solution will allow you to do everything you want to do with the data. But you should be aware of the limitations. When you push data out to other systems, you can typically only do so at the segment level. So while you have the data stored at the individual level within the CDP, you cannot pass it to other systems to use in machine-learning algorithms. Instead, you can create segments within the CDP and pass segment membership to outside systems to use for activation.

Passing data to outside systems also typically does not occur in real time. This is often acceptable for situations such as advertising, emails, push notifications, etc. But in situations where you want to respond to any information you have learned in real time, such as website or mobile app experiences as well as a call-center or in-store/in-branch interaction, real-time response is important.

When your CDP acts on the data to personalize experiences across channels, it can do so at the individual level and in real time. We'll get into a more complete conversation about personalization and CDP technology requirements in Chapter 8.

ELEMENTS OF GREAT DATA FOR PERSONALIZATION

Think back to how we described bad data at the beginning of the chapter. Data can be "bad" for personalization when it's inaccurate, outdated, insufficient or siloed. Good data, on the other hand, is:

Accurate: Can you rely on your data sources? Consider weighing the cost of using any inaccurate source against the benefit of the information it gives you.

Real-Time: Are you able to collect and act on your data in real time? Not all data needs to be real time, but some data could be outdated by the time it's used. Think through your real-time needs.

In-depth: Do you have enough data to fully understand each individual? You can get started with attributes and simple behavioral data, but truly individualized machine learning-driven experiences require in-depth data.

Modeled/Analyzed: Can you analyze the data to understand individual preferences and intent? Can you leverage predictive models to make assumptions about the future? Making the most of your data means more than just collecting it; it means making inferences to understand what it actually means about each individual.

Centralized and Actionable: Is all of your data in one customer data platform and usable by a personalization engine to deliver relevant experiences across channels? Most marketers have data siloed across their organization. Consider which data sources you need to deliver personalized experiences and how you can bring them together.

The foundation of any one-to-one marketing strategy is the customer data. When thinking about your own sources of information and marketing technology, the data aspect can seem daunting. But it's worth spending the time to find the right partners and data sources. Remember: bad data means bad personalization.

CHAPTER 4 ENDNOTES

39. Evergage Inc. and Researchscape International, "2019 Trends in Personalization," Apr 2019, http://www.evergage.com/resources/ebooks/ trends-in-personalization-survey-report/.

40. Forrester Consulting, "The Contextual Marketing Imperative: The Evolution Of Personalization From Push Messaging To One-To-One Personal Customer Experiences," Oct 2015, https://assets.cdn.sap.com/sapcom/ docs/2015/10/3c6868f1-487c-0010-82c7-eda71af511fa.pdf.

CHAPTER 5

CONSIDER THE FULL EXPERIENCE

Throughout the book, we've given examples of what's possible with personalization. In this chapter, we'll switch gears a little to go into more detail about the different forms and formats personalization can take. Once you have these basics under your belt, it will be much easier to understand what's achievable when planning your own personalization initiatives.

At the broadest level, there are two types of personalized experiences: interruptive and seamless.

Interruptive experiences are messages or content that a person does not necessarily expect to see and that are not integral to the current experience he is having. Many types of ads, emails and push notifications—as well as any web or app messages that overlay the existing page or screen—qualify as interruptive. For example, if you were to provide a pop-up message to visitors with personalized content based on their location, that pop-up sits on top of the rest of your site and is easily recognized as a separate personalized message.

Seamless experiences, in contrast, are usually indistinguishable from the existing default experience. Seamless experiences can include any type of content that is inserted, replaced, hidden or modified on a page or in-app. For example, if you personalize the headline or a CTA button on your landing page, that text and image are part of the page itself and blend in with the rest of the content. Any human-to-human experiences—such as any time a salesperson, call center agent or in-store associate interacts with a customer—would also qualify as seamless.

In the early days, personalization was limited to more interruptive and intrusive messages with an "in-your-face" approach, but the industry has moved toward more seamless personalization. That said, both have their benefits and should be selected based on your campaign objectives.

Let's get into the specifics.

INTERRUPTIVE EXPERIENCES

Interruptive experiences are best used when you want a message to grab someone's attention or encourage the person to take a specific action. The strength of this kind of approach is also its weakness, however. These hard-to-miss messages can quickly become annoying, so it's important to ensure that they are used sparingly and are as relevant as possible.

Creating more effective, less irritating interruptive experiences starts with understanding the forms they can take.

DIGITAL ADS

Some ad types can be considered interruptive, like pop-ups or interstitials, since they visually interrupt a visitor's experience. These ads ask visitors to stop what they were attempting to do to engage with ad content instead—and that can be a tough sell. We've all seen pop-ups across the internet that are irrelevant and annoying. As a result, ads like these are much less common than they were 10 to 20 years ago compared to more seamless ad types, but they certainly still exist.

PUSH NOTIFICATIONS

Delivered on mobile devices, push notifications are similar to interruptive ad formats: they pop up on a user's screen when he's not necessarily expecting them. They differ from ads, however, in that users typically opt in to receive them, and they're generally geared toward assisting users versus promoting products or offers. They can be sent to any person who has downloaded a mobile app—even when that app is not in use. Because they are used to interrupt any activity a person is currently engaged with on his phone or tablet, they should also be used sparingly. And, as we described in Chapter 3, they should leverage all the data a marketer has amassed from that person's usage of the app (or other channels when applicable) to ensure that he receives only relevant notifications.

OUTBOUND EMAIL

Outbound emails are those that a person did not opt-in to receive. While not an ideal marketing tactic, using such emails can be valuable under certain circumstances.

For example, outbound emails are often used by B2B marketers to drive traffic to their sponsored booths at trade shows. Marketers may receive a list of attending companies in advance, and if they are not given the names of attendees, they may use a combination of data sources as well as their judgment about which employees might attend. They may then send outbound emails to the people they have identified, leveraging effective messaging and incentives to encourage prospects to visit the company's booth.

In this situation, marketers know very little about the recipients: these people have not likely engaged with the company before. Therefore, it is not possible to leverage the personalization tactics we've described so far in the book. However, it is always a good idea to make the emails as relevant as possible. In this case, the content should be pertinent to the event as well as tailored to the attendee's industry and job title or role.

ONSITE AND IN-APP MESSAGES

Finally, there are the experiences that take place on a company's site or in its app. These are the messages that a marketer wants to ensure a visitor receives while engaging with the channel. Pop-ups, infobars and callouts are the most common types of interruptive onsite or in-app experiences. We'll walk through each of these in detail and provide ideal use cases and tips to make them relevant and effective.

POP-UPS

As opposed to creating indiscriminate pop-ups that contain advertisements, marketers can deliver pop-ups on their own sites and apps with messages for their own visitors and customers. Pop-ups tend to be very effective at catching someone's attention, because they typically need to be closed before the visitor can continue to view the page. But as we explained earlier, they can be intrusive to the overall site or app experience and should be used sparingly.

As innocuous as a pop-up may be, an irrelevant pop-up could cause someone to leave your site without engaging. But there are a few personalization strategies that you can use to help make your pop-ups more relevant and less intrusive:

Timing: Time a pop-up to display only when a user demonstrates certain behaviors such as scrolling down a page, showing intent to exit, spending a certain amount of time on a page, or clicking a specific link.

Individualized Content: Tailor the message content to the individual's preferences or affinities. For example, an exit message (one that displays when a visitor is about to leave the site) could display a product that a shopper showed intent to purchase in the

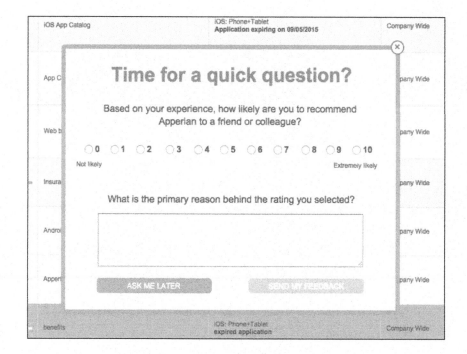

Pop-up within a web app displaying an NPS survey

session or an eBook not yet downloaded by a B2B visitor but specific to her interests. With this degree of relevance, you maximize your odds of re-engaging the visitor.

Contextual Targeting: Target your messages to visitors based on their referral source, location, device type or other attribute. When the message incorporates a relevant frame of reference, it is more compelling and engaging.

Lightbox Effect: If the information you're looking to convey with a pop-up is particularly important, a lightbox effect (also called a "modal")—which grays out the rest of the page—is a good way to focus the visitor's attention on your message and desired action.

Here are a few key use cases for personalized pop-ups:

Exit Message: A retailer may display a pop-up message that features products a shopper has left in his cart, perhaps reminding him of any incentives that are available to him, to encourage him to purchase before he leaves.

Email Capture: A B2B site focused on demand generation may display a pop-up to an engaged reader of its blog, encouraging her to sign up for the newsletter if she hasn't yet done so.

Alert: A financial services site may display a pop-up when a visitor tries to abandon a credit card application, reminding her that her work will not be saved

Clearly, pop-ups should be used judiciously on your site or in your app. As you plan new pop-ups, make sure to evaluate your existing experience to ensure that you don't have too many pop-ups running at once. And always test your pop-ups to determine if they're effective. Consider trying different copy, images, CTAs or message types if you don't see the impact you expected.

INFOBARS

Infobars are designed to capture a visitor's attention by appearing at the top or bottom of a page. They persist as "sticky" messages that remain on the top or bottom of the user's screen when scrolling, but they can be designed to be easily closed or dismissed.

Infobars are ideal for reminders, such as for upcoming sales or new content assets. They can either contain a simple informational message or a CTA that directs visitors to a specific page for more detail. While many sites use infobars to give reminders to all site visitors, messages can be tailored to each individual's attributes or behaviors. Here are some examples:

Free Shipping/Loyalty Points: A retailer may want to use an infobar to alert a shopper that he qualifies for free shipping or has loyalty points to use. That message will appear on any page he visits but will not be obtrusive.

Webinar/Tradeshow/Content Registration: A technology provider may want to display an infobar to promote an upcoming webinar only to visitors within a specific industry, to alert visitors of upcoming events in their area, or to announce new eBooks or white papers that may be relevant to them.

Upsell: An insurance site could display an infobar to subtly inform a customer that she qualifies for reduced rates on auto insurance when bundled with the home insurance she already has with that company.

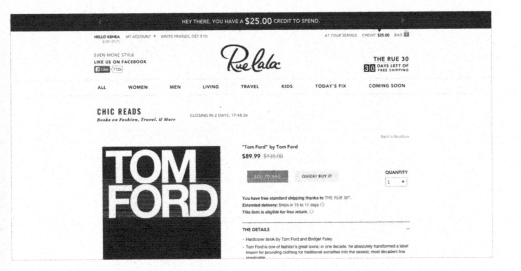

Infobar on top of page displays a shopper's remaining credits

While it's clear that infobars are not as obtrusive as pop-ups, it's important to test each infobar to determine its effectiveness. When in doubt, it's a good idea to test the same message using other formats to see which works best.

CALLOUTS

Generally smaller and less conspicuous than other message formats, callouts draw attention to a particular area or feature within a page. We often see these used within web apps to point out a product's new features or to ask users to take a tour, but they can be employed anytime you want to call attention to a page element.

There are many ways to incorporate callouts into the experience while providing value to the visitor. Here are some examples:

Ask for reviews: A retailer could display a callout around a product asking a shopper who purchased the product to review it.

Direct to help content or FAQs: A technology provider could display a callout to customers who appear to be struggling within its product and direct them to the appropriate help content or FAQ.

Indicate a new or unused feature: A financial services site could display a callout to indicate a new feature within its account management tools or could call out a feature the customer has not yet used.

As with pop-ups and infobars, you can display a callout to anyone that visits a particular page—making it a non-personalized callout. But there are several ways to tailor callouts to make them a bit more sophisticated and relevant to specific visitors. Some examples:

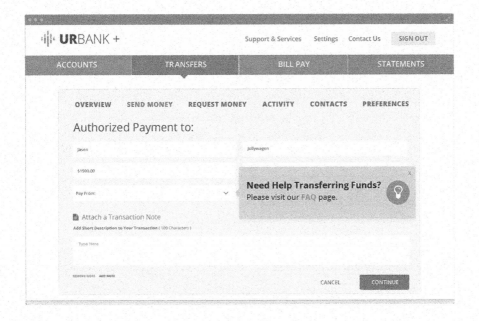

Callout asks customers if they need help transferring funds

Target newbies: Segment your audience so that only first-time users or those who have never engaged with a specific feature see the message.

Time on idle: Time the callout so that it only appears when a visitor's mouse is idle for several seconds, and use the message to provide assistance, additional detail or motivation.

Time on hover: Time the callout to display only when a visitor's mouse is near the intended area of the page or hovers over the specific feature being called out.

As with all messages and experiences, testing callout messages is critical. Test out different designs and copy to find the most effective option for your site or app. Similar to pop-ups, callouts should be used sparingly, as having multiple messages appear on the page whenever a visitor moves her mouse can be disorienting.

SEAMLESS EXPERIENCES

In contrast to the above-described interruptive formats, which are easily distinguishable from the rest of the customer's experience, seamless experiences are an integral part of the experience and are often expected by the visitor or recipient.

INLINE ADS

Seamless advertising formats such as banner, search and social ads are more commonly seen these days than interruptive formats like pop-ups. These are the ads that appear as "sponsored" posts on Facebook or LinkedIn or along the edges (or in the middle) of articles on media sites. They do not interrupt the experience, but they're typically labeled as advertisements in some way. These types of ads generally provide a better experience for visitors, as they do not physically block visitors from interacting with the page's content.

Advertisers often leverage retargeting in their inline ads, relying on a person's past website visit behavior to deliver more relevant content. But as we described back in Chapter 3, advertisers often use limited data to target these ads, resulting in less-than-relevant experiences. Using more detailed behavioral data and other data stored in the CDP to understand what a person was truly engaged with (or even predict what their future needs will be) results in more appropriate personalization and more effective retargeting.

OPT-IN EMAIL

Since a person has to provide his email address to receive opt-in emails, this format is considered a seamless rather than an interruptive experience. There are three key types of opt-in emails:

Transactional Email: Transactional emails are sent after a person takes an action, such as placing an order or subscribing to a newsletter. These emails, which are expected by the recipients, are often a great place to deliver personalized content to drive upsells or deeper engagement. For example, using everything you know about a shopper's preferences, you can recommend products she may like after she has purchased a pair of shoes.

Triggered Email: While less expected than transactional emails, triggered emails can be considered seamless experiences as well. As we described in Chapter 3, triggered emails are often used to remind shoppers of abandoned carts, but they can also be used to encourage shoppers to purchase products they were highly

Triggered cart abandonment email includes individualized
product recommendations

engaged with during a session. Or, they can be used to prompt visitors to take key, uncompleted actions in an app or to carry out the next step in an onboarding sequence. The content inside triggered emails should be personalized to every individual so that users find something relevant, meaningful and helpful in the message.

Ongoing Email: Finally, ongoing emails are a mainstay for nearly all companies. Retailers update their shoppers on the latest sales and promotions, media companies provide the latest news and information to their subscribers, financial institutions keep their clients informed about market trends, and B2B companies provide helpful guides and resources as part of their content marketing strategies. These may include large-scale "batch and blast" email campaigns or narrower segment-based communications. B2B companies often employ "nurture" marketing, a more sophisticated form of ongoing email marketing. For example, if a prospect downloads certain content or signs up for a webinar, he is put into a segment or "track" and receives ongoing, helpful information relevant to his areas of interest.

Ongoing emails, including nurture emails, are not usually tied to recipients' behaviors on web or mobile, but they can and should be. They may be personalized using "mail merge" techniques to include first name or company name in the subject line or body of the email, but that's a minimal level of personalization. Any action a person takes on the company website can be used to build upon her individual profile, and the data should be leveraged to personalize ongoing email communications using open-time personalization (covered in Chapter 3). For example, if a visitor already downloaded an eBook or viewed a blog post, she does not need to be sent the content again in an email. She should receive something more relevant, determined at open time, instead.

*In-page edit replaces relevant content recommendation directly into the
site navigation for different industry segments*

SEAMLESS WEBSITE AND IN-APP EXPERIENCES

As with interruptive formats, seamless formats can be used both on websites and within apps. Seamless format types appear to be a part of the page itself, although they're actually delivered through a personalization platform by inserting, replacing, hiding or modifying content. Visitors should not realize that what they're seeing is personalized: the content should always blend into the existing page and never flicker.

The two main types of seamless personalization are in-page edits and inline content. While they are very similar, there is a distinct difference.

IN-PAGE EDITS

In-page edits refer to any changes made to existing hard-coded content on a page—whether that content is modified or hidden completely. This allows you to make subtle yet impactful changes to your website to appeal to different visitors and make them feel that your website is intuitively relevant to them.

Examples of in-page edits are essentially unlimited; marketers can usually identify numerous ways to personalize their websites from a quick brainstorming session. Here are a few to get you started:

> **Homepage Heroes:** Inserting in-page edits to the homepage hero experience is a compelling use case for companies across industries. It is one of the easiest ways to ensure that your homepage is relevant to any of your major personas or segments to reduce homepage bounce and encourage deeper engagement. A B2B demand generation site could leverage an ABM approach to deliver a different homepage image and copy to

each of its target industries. A retail site could display a different homepage experience for visitors who have shopped certain product categories. A financial services site could deliver different homepage images and copy for target personas such as students, homeowners or veterans.

CTAs: CTAs are often tested extensively, but tend to remain static for all visitors. A demand generation site could display a different CTA for different industries or different stages of the funnel (such as "Explore Financial Services Solutions" versus "Explore Healthcare Solutions," or "Download this Retail eBook" versus "Download this Insurance eBook"). Taking it a step further, the company could even change the CTA after someone has already taken the action to be maximally relevant.

Site Navigation: In-page edits are not limited to page content itself. You can change a site or app's navigation for different groups of visitors, such as in the Dyn case study we shared several chapters ago.

Irrelevant Information: A personalized experience can even include hiding content that is irrelevant to a particular segment or visitor. For example, a retail site could remove a mention of free domestic shipping for international visitors, or a blog site could remove a section that encourages subscription to a newsletter if the visitor has already done so.

INLINE CONTENT

While in-page edits allow you to edit or hide content that is hard-coded on a page, inline content enables you to dynamically *add* full sections of content to a page. In most cases, visitors will not notice that any personalization is occurring or that a new section has been added; the content blends in. Essentially, inline content provides a seamless way to display information to visitors within the context and construct of the page.

There are many reasons why you may want to add something specific to a page for a group or individual. Some examples:

Free Shipping: An e-commerce site could insert inline content directly onto its cart page to encourage shoppers to buy more to qualify for free shipping. The site can even include product recommendations that would qualify the shopper for free shipping. Visitors who already qualify for free shipping could be shown something else in the same space, or the space could be blank without affecting the look of the site.

Upcoming Webinars: A B2B company focused on demand generation could include an invite shown to select visitors for an upcoming webinar on its webinar recordings page, inserted at the top of the page. If that visitor does not qualify or has already registered, or if there are no upcoming webinars, no such content would appear.

You may realize that these examples could easily be interruptive message types as well. Think about the webinar example from just above. The B2B site could highlight its latest webinar in an infobar at the top of the page, or as a callout as a visitor's mouse hovered over a specific section of the website. The difference is that in these examples, the message is a part of the site experience itself, rather than imposing on it.

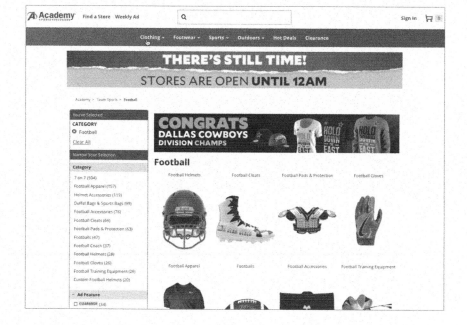

"Dallas Cowboys" message inserted into page as an inline message
when relevant to certain shoppers

PICKING FORMATS

Of all the formats available, which is the "correct" one to choose? There is, of course, no right answer to the question. Different messages will lend themselves better to different formats, and there will be many occasions where you will have to make a judgment about which format best fits the situation, your brand and your customers' expectations. That is why testing is so critical (and we'll get into it in Chapter 6).

Broadly, however, it's important to note that seamless experiences allow you to do more with personalization. It's not a good idea, for example, to personalize your website using only pop-ups. Using in-page and inline content, you can subtly tailor the full site experience to each individual. That means taking full advantage of the machine-learning algorithms we outlined in Chapter 2 and of all of the data types we detailed last chapter. You can use these resources to provide recommendations for products, brands, content and categories; to personalize list sorting; to dynamically modify site navigation; and to otherwise provide well-rounded and fully personalized experiences. You can't do all of that with pop-ups alone. Technology has come so far since the days of Peppers and Rogers, and you no longer need to limit personalization to interruptive formats or prescribed locations on your site.

We found in our annual study that email campaigns, homepages and landing pages are the most common areas where marketers leverage personalization.[41] We have brought up each of these campaign types in this book, and they are each extremely valuable. But to provide a fully personalized experience that exists no matter which page a visitor is on or which channel she uses, marketers can expand their personalization efforts to include additional pages, search results, navigation and more.

Of course, while it's completely possible to dive headfirst into full-experience personalization, it's not necessary to do so. We have seen a number of marketers who start with interruptive message types and basic seamless experiences targeted to broad segments when they begin personalizing, but who then evolve to more sophisticated tactics. A case study illustrates this here.

CASE STUDY: SHOELINE.COM

Several years ago, Shoeline.com, an online shoe retailer, began leveraging personalization on its website. At the start of its personalization journey, the company was primarily focused on capturing email addresses and offering incentives to visitors based on referral source. For example, it designed a lightbox-style pop-up for shoppers arriving from a Google search. The pop-up included the product that was searched for and provided a discount to create urgency to convert.

After testing the power of personalization and achieving a number of quick wins with several similar campaigns, Shoeline wanted to do more. It began to design more seamless experiences that leveraged individual shopper intent in the moment. Some examples include:

• Personalized homepage experiences display copy based on the shoe category shoppers have spent the most time engaging with both in the current session and over time. Some of these shoe categories are relevant to very specific groups and not at all to others. This campaign allows Shoeline to promote more niche categories on its homepage without risking irrelevance to many of its shoppers. If a shopper never engaged with nursing shoes, for example, she would never see that category on the homepage.
• A personalized shopping companion provides shoppers with easy access to the products with which they were most engaged or which they had previously purchased. The

contents of the tab are completely personalized for each person, and products are sorted based on level of engagement with each product in past and current sessions.
• Individualized recommendations across product and category pages leverage boosters to individualize recommendations based on shoppers' affinities, helping them discover shoes they are most likely to purchase.

Personalized experiences on Shoeline.com have improved product discovery for visitors and driven increased conversions. While clickthroughs of its generic homepage banner were typically around 1%, the site's personalized banners—targeted to key shopper personas—achieved clickthroughs up to an incredible 26%. And for visitors who engaged with the personalized shopping companion, Shoeline saw a conversion rate of 18%, which is a remarkable seven times higher than the average site-wide conversion rate.

Both interruptive and seamless personalization have their place in a successful personalization strategy, but seamless personalization across the full customer experience is the way of the future. Like Shoeline.com, companies sometimes start with simple interruptive messages to dip their toes in the water before making personalization a fundamental site component, with more elaborate inline and in-page content.

Generally speaking, with personalization across channels, we're seeing an increased focus on building a relationship with the customer, not just catching their attention with something relevant. This means focusing on what will actually be beneficial to each person. In the same vein, many marketers are moving from batch-

Shoeline.com's homepage experience for visitors with an affinity for nursing shoes

and-blast generic emails to 1-to-1 triggered emails that are more relevant to each recipient in the moment. And they're moving from reaching broad audiences with digital advertising to reaching highly targeted, narrow audiences.

Marketers are finding that using personalization tactics that are seamless, helpful and timely are the best ways to improve the end customer experience and have the most impact on their businesses over time.

CHAPTER 5 ENDNOTES

41. Evergage Inc. and Researchscape International, "2019 Trends in Personalization," Apr 2019, http://www.evergage.com/resources/ebooks/ trends-in-personalization-survey-report/.

CHAPTER 6

TESTING, ANALYTICS AND ROI

Nearly every marketer, across industries, is faced with the challenge of juggling multiple priorities with limited resources. There is always more to do than seems possible. As a result, good marketing is a balancing act. Any decision a marketing team makes to pursue a particular strategy, tactic or campaign has to be weighed against other potential investments.

At the same time, measuring the ROI of marketing activities isn't always easy. Not every campaign or activity—such as the many tactics marketers use to influence "awareness" or to provide "market education"—can be cleanly tied back to a business metric. These activities are often critical to the overall business, but they can be tricky or impossible to measure. As a result, marketers don't always know whether the choices they make have real impact.

This measurement challenge also exists for marketing technology decisions. As a marketer, you want to invest in the tools that will be most effective for your organization. However, the range of marketing technology ("martech") solutions on the market seems to grow by the minute. Scott Brinker's yearly marketing technology graphic in 2019 included 7,040 solutions—up from 6,829 in 2018 and 3,874 in 2017.[42] Most marketers are using some combination of these 7,000-plus solutions—sometimes as many as 20 to 50—to accomplish their goals.[43] No wonder Hubspot found that proving the ROI of marketing activities is the second greatest challenge facing marketers today (after generating traffic).[44] When you stitch together a bunch of solutions to address a variety of needs, it can be nearly impossible to connect your efforts to your company's bottom line or to assess the value of each individual technology investment.

But personalization isn't just another marketing tactic, and it shouldn't just be about adding another solution to your tech stack. If you've taken anything away from this book so far, it should be that personalization can and should fundamentally change the customer experience for your company. It can help you show your customers and prospects that you understand them at the individual level. This is critical in today's world, where catching someone's attention—not to mention keeping that attention—can be a herculean task.

In this chapter, we'll get into the importance of testing in personalization, how it works, and how it directly relates to calculating ROI. Testing all your personalization campaigns not only allows you to find the campaigns that perform best, but also to quantify the impact of your personalization efforts on your KPIs to ensure you're making the most of your investments.

A/B TESTING

Most marketers are familiar with testing and often use it for optimizing email subject lines, landing pages, digital advertising copy and more across digital and offline channels. Without testing the approaches and tactics they're currently using, marketers would never know what's working or what could be improved.

When it comes to personalization, testing can help you understand when a collaborative filtering algorithm is more effective than a co-browse algorithm for a specific group, or when an inline message is more effective than a call-out. It can also tell you whether a particular personalization campaign is more or less effective for certain visitor segments, or whether it's best to reach an individual via email or push notification. Much like other marketing tactics, you don't know what types of personalized experiences will work or if they're optimized until you test your ideas. What works for one site, app or email may not necessarily work for another.

Employing testing on your personalization campaigns can help you find what works best for your own business and channels. Also called split testing, A/B testing is the most common form of testing that we see. With A/B testing, you typically split your site traffic into two groups: an "A" experience for one group, and a "B" experience for another. The experience that drives the best results is the winner. The same concept, of course, can be applied to three or more groups, which is why it is sometimes also referred to as A/B/n testing.

Let's look at an example. As a retailer you may want to know if, on a product detail page for a pair of boots, it is more effective to show recommendations for similar styles or to display recommendations from other categories to "complete the look." Is a product carousel more effective than no carousel? Should there be three product recommendations on the page or four? Or, in another example, is it more effective to recommend a blog post to a visitor via an interruptive message that slides in from the side, or with an inline section inserted right into the post being viewed? An A/B test can help you understand which works best for your site, app and audiences.

Typically, when marketers who do not yet use personalization utilize A/B testing, they do so to find the best-performing experience for *all* of their traffic. This approach helps them figure out which experience appeals most to the least common denominator. But, as we've discussed, one-size-fits-all experiences are quickly becoming a thing of the past. A/B testing needs to be combined with personalization to be maximally effective.

USING A CONTROL

One of the most important components of any personalization test is a control—or the default (non-personalized) experience. For example, if you're testing an algorithm to provide product or content recommendations directly in a search bar, you might want to test some portion of the traffic with one version of the algorithm (experience A), some portion of the traffic with another version (experience B), and the remaining portion with no personalized search at all (experience C). In this case, C is the control group. You could also test one version of the algorithm (experience A) against a control to determine if the personalized experience outperforms a generic one, and then test different versions of the algorithm against A going forward to find the most effective one. (Just remember that the more experiences you test at once, the longer it will take to achieve statistically significant results.)

When testing personalized experiences, including a control is critical because you always want to be sure that personalization outperforms a generic experience. It is possible that your idea missed the mark for the segment you targeted, or that your personalized experience was confusing to visitors. Measuring against a control will help uncover these findings.

Keep in mind, however, that even if you find that there is no difference between a control and test experience—or even that a generic experience outperforms a personalized one—that doesn't mean that personalization does not work. It could simply mean that you need to find a more effective personalization strategy for that particular use case.

CASE STUDY: EVERGAGE

At Evergage, we discovered a situation in which a test against a control group told us we were not providing a sufficiently effective personalized experience. We were using a feature called "SmartHistory" to display a tab at the side of each visitor's screen that provided easy access to content (eBooks, case studies, etc.) the visitor had previously engaged with or downloaded on the site.

For the test we conducted, a portion of our traffic saw

a blue tab on the right side of their screen labeled "SmartHistory," while the control group did not have this feature. For the target group, all content they had viewed or downloaded appeared in the SmartHistory tab, sorted by how much they engaged with each piece of content. For example, if a visitor clicked on a data sheet and spent three minutes on the page, and a case study, where she only spent a couple of seconds, the data sheet would appear first in SmartHistory, and the case study, second.

We thought this would improve visitor experience and increase conversions, but when we examined the test results, we were not able to find a statistically significant difference in website conversions between those who had the SmartHistory tab and those who did not.

Instead of assuming that personalization was ineffective, we decided to tweak our approach. We added another experience to our test, splitting our traffic into three groups: one that saw the original SmartHistory tab, one that saw a tab with a different, more intuitive label ("Your Downloads"), and one that saw no tab (a control group).

This time, we found our winner. Our new experience resulted in a remarkable 69% lift in website conversions over the control. And, of course, the "Your Downloads" version beat out the original SmartHistory tab as well.

MEASURING AGAINST MULTIPLE METRICS

Another important consideration for A/B testing is deciding which metric to look at. With any campaign, you should have a specific metric or two in mind that you would like to improve. Testing the campaign against these metrics ensures that you are moving in the right direction. For example, if you run an email capture campaign, you probably want to grow the number of email addresses you collect. If you

Evergage's "Your Downloads" tab helps visitors find recently
viewed content.

deliver product recommendations across your site, you probably want to measure the effect on conversion rate. If you run a direct mail campaign, you may want to drive traffic to your branch locations. Any test you run for a campaign should help you understand which approach will have the largest impact on those metrics.

However, no campaign operates in isolation. It is very common to affect multiple metrics with one campaign. Thus, it is possible for a campaign to increase conversions but decrease average order value (for example, through a campaign that drives visitors to purchase lower priced items). If average order value decreases too much, it could actually have a negative impact on revenues even if the conversion rate improves. An email capture campaign could gather hundreds of extra email addresses, yet cause the site bounce rate to increase dramatically—leading to a decrease in engaged visitors. A marketer needs to consider all of this information to determine whether such campaigns were successes or failures.

To understand the full impact of any personalization campaign, you must measure it against the narrow goals for your campaign, as well as your global goals. Define your overall business goals (e.g., form completions, sign-ups, purchases, lifetime value, retention etc.) and analyze any campaign's results against these objectives to determine a campaign's positive or negative impact on your primary business objectives.

HAVING CONFIDENCE IN YOUR RESULTS

Advanced testers are probably familiar with what the results of an A/B test mean, but others can struggle to understand what the numbers are really saying. It's important to know what your results mean so you can make the right decision about how to proceed after the test.

Testing tools can use different statistical approaches, so you'll want to understand the basics of your specific solution. Most solutions do not predict the lifts you'll see when you convert all of your traffic to the test experience—those results will ultimately be higher or lower than what you saw during the test. Instead, the results are telling you that you can be X% confident (typically 95%) that the test experience will beat the control experience. Some solutions can predict an interval of the lift you can expect when the test ends, but it's important to keep in mind that just because you saw a 5% lift in conversion rate during the test, it does not mean that you will experience that exact lift going forward.

For example, look at the image on the next page. It depicts a test of a redesign vs. a control experience. It shows that, at the current point in the test, the redesign is delivering a lift in revenue per user (RPU) of 32.4% over the control experience at 95% confidence.

This *does not mean* that we can be 95% sure that you'll receive a 32.4% lift in RPU when you end the test and allow 100% of your traffic to see the redesigned experience. It just means that you can be confident that the redesigned experience beats the control experience to a meaningful extent.

MULTIVARIATE TESTING

The insights gained from A/B testing can be extremely valuable, but the approach only allows you to test one variable at a time. Multivariate testing (MVT), on the other hand, allows you to simultaneously test multiple aspects of a personalized experience—including text, graphics, formats, styles, and more—to determine the best combination of changes to achieve a desired outcome.

For example, suppose you are uncertain which header (Header 1 or Header 2) and footer (Footer 1 or Footer 2) combination on your company's website is the most effective at driving leads. Using MVT, you can simultaneously test these options to determine which combination works best.

One important caveat is that because an MVT campaign will split traffic across all of your potential combinations, it may take some extra

Positive Outcome

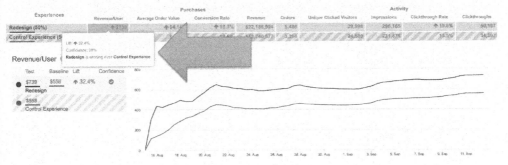

*At this point in the test, the redesign is delivering a lift in RPU of
32.4% over the control experience.*

HEADER SECTION	FOOTER SECTION
Header 1	Footer 1
Header 2	Footer 2

Using multivariate testing, you can test the combination of these options to determine which works best.

time and traffic to reach statistical significance (depending on the amount of traffic you have on your site). For example, with a 50/50 A/B test and a 10% control, 45% of your users will see Test A, 45% will see Test B, and 10% will see nothing. But a four-combination multivariate test with a 10% control (as in the above example) will mean that only 22.5% of your audience will see each combination. Additionally, it is difficult to identify in an MVT test when one section of the test impacts conversion, but the other parts do not. For example, let's say that the combination of Header 1 and Footer 1 is the winner. With an MVT test, there is no way of knowing whether the header or footer is driving the results.

So when would you use an A/B test and when would you use an MVT test? The typical rule of thumb is that you should use an A/B test for major changes, such as the layout of a page, and an MVT test to fine- tune page elements to ensure that they all work together. Thus, an A/B test is ideal for testing a hypothesis when you're seeking a specific answer to a question. For example, if you think that one experience would perform better as an inline message rather than a pop-up, you can run an A/B test to find out. Or, to determine if your shoppers are particularly brand loyal, you could test one algorithm for product recommendations that boosts brand preference against one that does not. Once you have defined which personalized elements work best, you can test all of those elements together with MVT to determine the most effective combination.

TESTING TIPS

Testing sounds easier than it is. You simply pick a few experiences, set them up, and run them against each other and a control to see what performs best. But it can often be more complex than that. What should you test? What do you do if a test did not go well? Here are a few general testing tips to give you more guidance.

HAVE A CLEAR PURPOSE AND THINK THROUGH THE IMPACT

A poorly designed test can be confusing at best and harmful at worst if you don't know what you're testing for. The key is to have a testable assertion and the right control group to compare your hypothesis against. If you're not sure what you're testing, you may not be able to learn anything from the result.

It's also worth thinking through the potential negative impacts of any campaign in advance (and getting any necessary approvals when appropriate). That way, if you see any negative effects during the test, you'll be able to know when to stop the test before too much damage occurs. Some testers opt to keep testing samples low at first when a negative impact is a concern.

DETERMINE YOUR TEST DURATION BY YOUR BUSINESS CYCLE

Most businesses see dramatic shifts in site activity depending on the day. Many B2B sites see the bulk of their traffic during the week—with a drop off on the weekends. Retailers may see traffic peaks during nights and weekends. With that in mind, it doesn't make sense to run a test from Thursday to Sunday on any given week, because the results won't control for any changes in behavior from the beginning of the week to the end. It also wouldn't make sense to run a test for a week and a half (for example, beginning a test on Monday and ending it on Wednesday of the following week) because the results will reflect two Mondays, two Tuesdays and two Wednesdays but only one Thursday, one Friday, etc. This will skew the results.

A good rule of thumb is never to run a test for less than a week — to ensure you see each day of the week reflected in the data — and to run tests for multiples of a full week.

However, some businesses may want to run longer tests if they have highly variable monthly activity. For example, if you have a subscription-based business where the subscriptions all renew at the end of the month, you may want to run a test for at least a full month to ensure you control for behavioral patterns unique to your business.

LET THE CAMPAIGN RUN

It can be tempting to end a test early if it's not showing you the results you expected (or to declare victory too early), but some campaigns take longer to take effect for a number of reasons. It's important to keep the test running until those that see the experience are able to act on it.

CASE STUDY: RETAILER

A retailer offered a promotion for $15 off a minimum purchase of $100. This $100 purchase was higher than the site's average order value (AOV) of $75. In this test, the retailer was trying to increase AOV.

The retailer found that it took some time from when a person saw the offer to when he or she actually acted on it. Looking at users who acted within the first hour of seeing the message, the control outperformed the experiment. In other words, those who didn't see the message converted at a higher rate than those who saw the message. But over time, conversions increased among those who saw the offer. You can view the results in the graphic that follows.

We can theorize that the offer in the case study took some time to take effect because the minimum order value was much higher than the AOV on the site. Shoppers needed some time to think about the purchase and identify how they would spend more to reach the minimum. So while the offer didn't produce a conversion in the same session, but it affected conversions over time and ultimately did boost AOV.

In cases like this one, it's important to keep the test running. A good understanding of how to do proper A/B testing—in conjunction with an understanding of your own site—should help you apply the best judgment in this area.

FILTER THE RESULTS

We all know that in life, something new can grab our attention simply because it's new, not because it's better than the old. And with limited attention spans, that excitement over the "new thing" wears off fast. The same can be true with digital experiences. A new experience can produce greater engagement compared to an old experience just because visitors are not used to seeing it. When reviewing test results, make sure you identify whether any positive results could simply be due to novelty.

One easy way to test this is to segment the results by new vs. returning visitors. If you see that a campaign is producing a strong positive effect with returning visitors and not with new visitors, it's highly likely that returning visitors are drawn to the novelty of the new experience and the results you're seeing will not last forever.

Of course, just because a campaign is doing well due to the novelty effect isn't necessarily a reason not to go forward with it. It just means that you should recognize that while you may see an initial bump, it isn't a long-term effect. At this point, it's a judgment call you need to make about whether that aligns with your goals. If you're testing a promotion on a retail site that will soon be replaced with a

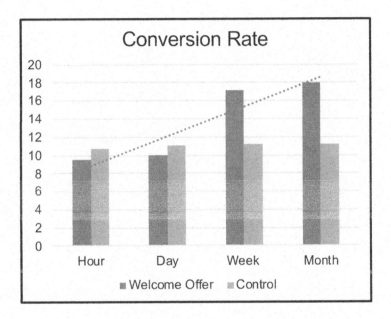

*In this test, it took some time before users who saw
the test acted on the promotion.*

new promotion, novelty is good. If you're testing a redesigned site experience that you expect will boost your metrics over the long term, this may not be what you're looking for.

WHEN IN DOUBT, TEST AGAIN

If there is any confusion as to whether a test was successful, don't hesitate to test it again. If you can't replicate the results, it may not have been a well-designed test. Don't forget to retest long-running campaigns as well, as circumstances may have changed since the initial test.

COMBINING A/B TESTING AND PERSONALIZATION

Let's revisit a concept we mentioned at the beginning of this chapter: While traditional A/B testing remains important, its true potential lies in its use in conjunction with personalization. A simple example can help illustrate.

Assume you're testing two different website experiences. We'll call them Experience A and Experience B. If you ran a traditional A/B test, you may see results like those on the next page. Let's assume the Y axis represents an important KPI to your business such as revenue per user, conversion rate, sign-ups, clickthroughs, etc.

These results tell us that Experience A clearly performs better than Experience B. Knowing this information, and assuming the results are statistically significant, you would set 100% of your traffic to see Experience A and move on to your next test.

But let's also assume that you have two audience segments, such as new visitors and return visitors. Let's call them Segment 1 and Segment 2. Each segment is of equal size, and each segment

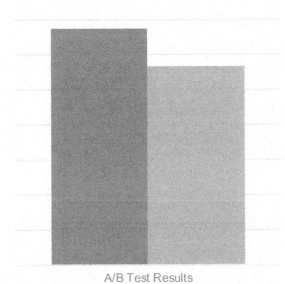

A/B Test Results

■ Experience 1   ■ Experience 2

Experience A clearly outperforms Experience B in this test.

responds differently to the tested experiences. If you broke down your test results by segment, you may see results like those on the next page.

These results show that Segment 1 responds better to Experience B, while Segment 2 responds better to Experience A. This is something we wouldn't know from looking at the results shown in the first graph, because we were looking at an *average* of how each segment responds to each experience. Both Segment 1's and Segment 2's reactions to Experience A and Experience B are averaged together to produce your overall performance numbers for those experiences, as illustrated on page 139. Clearly, that average hides some really interesting differences in the preferences of these segments.

Without personalization, even if you broke down the test results like this, you would still end up picking Experience A as the winner. After all, if you have to pick one single experience that is best for all, Experience A would be it. But by selecting Experience A, you're missing out on the additional benefit of showing Experience B to Segment 1.

With basic segment-based personalization, however, you wouldn't need to pick one experience over another. You can pick Experience A for Segment 2 and Experience B for Segment 1. In other words, you can choose the experience that "wins" for each segment, not just the experience that wins overall. Page 141 shows what it would look like if you stacked the results of the optimal experience for each segment compared to the optimal experience for all.

This is, of course, a highly simplified example. In reality, there is an unlimited number of ways you can segment your audience, and your segments will naturally vary in size. But the important thing to take away from this example is that just because a test produced a winning experience, it doesn't mean that experience is

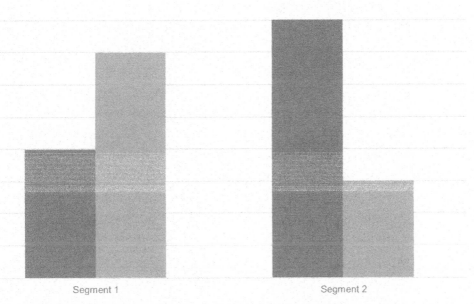

Each segment responds differently to the test experiences. Segment 1 prefers Experience B, while Segment 2 prefers Experience A.

the best for *everyone*. It just means it's the best you can do without personalization.

All of your traditional A/B tests are likely hiding critical information like this simplified example showed. It doesn't make sense to miss out on the unrealized benefits when you could just combine your A/B testing with personalization to deliver something relevant to everyone.

We're not suggesting that the overall principles of A/B testing don't still apply in a personalized world. There are just a few adjustments you need to make.

Rather than running tests to come up with one single best experience for all visitors, identify your most important segments and test different experiences for each one. B2B companies may segment by industry or company size (small business, enterprise, etc.). B2C retailers may segment by favorite category or preferred gender. Financial services companies may segment by products used (credit card, auto insurance, mortgage, etc.) or stage of life (student, new homebuyer, etc.). You can test several experiences for each of your key segments to find the experience that works best for each one.

And any time you run a test, always filter the results for different segments. You may find that a particular rule-based experience is yielding good results, but if you dig deeper, you may see that it performs better for loyal vs. occasional shoppers, for example.

You can also use machine learning as a powerful complement or alternative to traditional A/B testing, as we'll describe in the next section.

ELEVATE YOUR TESTING WITH MACHINE LEARNING AND PREDICTIVE SCORING

Now that we've gone into detail on A/B testing, the importance of combining it with personalization, and how to measure and analyze

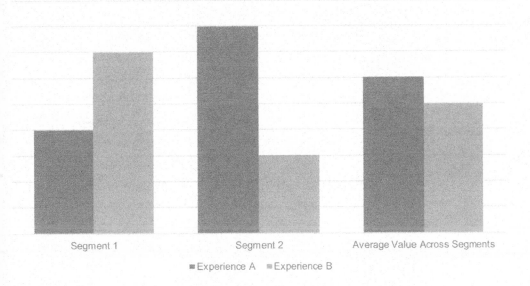

Segment 1   Segment 2   Average Value Across Segments

■ Experience A   ■ Experience B

Valuable information about your segments can be hiding in your
overall A/B test results.

your results, let's explore the impact of machine learning on testing and analytics. Machine learning offers significant current and future opportunities to elevate your testing and data analysis efforts.

PERSONALIZATION VIA CONTINUOUS LEARNING

As we've described, A/B testing was primarily designed to give you a single answer. If you want to test various aspects of your branding (such as fonts, colors, logos or taglines), site design, pricing, etc., you'll want to use A/B or multivariate testing because you don't plan to tailor the experience to different groups or individuals. You expect to find a single solution that beats out your other options.

But that's not necessarily your goal with personalization. If you have two different promotions to feature on your homepage, for example, A/B testing is designed to tell you which of the two options has the broadest appeal with some measure of confidence. But that's not truly your goal as a marketer. In reality, your goal is to derive the most business value from the two options. A/B testing cannot address that goal. You could get closer to that goal by selecting a few segments you think will react differently to the promotions, and use rules to target the promotions accordingly. But even then, you still aren't truly addressing your goal of getting maximum value out of each promotion—because no situation will be as simplistic as the example in the previous section.

A machine-learning algorithm, such as Contextual Bandit which we referenced back in Chapter 2, *can* address this goal. Contextual Bandit uses predictive scoring and machine learning to evaluate the probability of a person engaging with different promotions, images, offers or other experiences. A marketer can give the algorithm several different experiences to display in a specific area of the website or an email, and it will select the best one (with the highest value or lowest cost to the business) for each individual visitor.

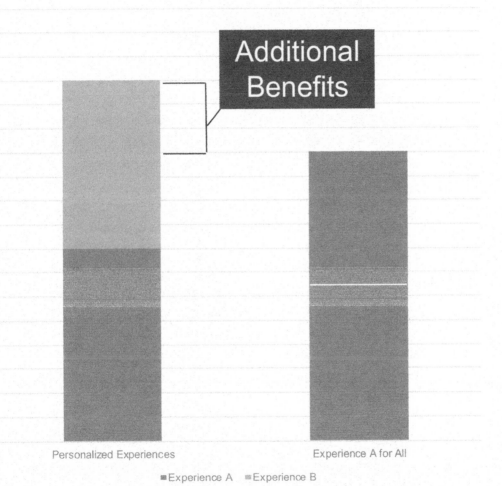

Additional Benefits

Personalized Experiences   Experience A for All

■Experience A   ■Experience B

By not personalizing, you're missing out on the additional benefit of
showing Experience B to Segment 1.

For example, if a company has 15 different homepage hero images it could potentially show a visitor, the algorithm considers all the data available about the person, factors in the value of someone converting on each image (clickthrough, offer acceptance, purchase, etc.) and makes the best choice for that person at that point in time.

The Contextual Bandit algorithm has two main benefits: individual-level personalization and continuous learning. Since we've already covered the value of one-to-one personalization in this book, let's spend a little more time on the continuous learning aspect.

When you run an A/B test, you have to let the test run for some period of time. During that time, some portion of your traffic will be viewing what will ultimately be determined the "losing" experience. You don't receive the full benefit of the winning experience until you end the test.

But Contextual Bandit is always learning and improving. You do not need to wait for a test to end to analyze the results, because it will automatically incorporate anything it has learned going forward. It can learn how different types of people interact with your site or emails that it would take marketers a long time to uncover through the data (if they ever do) and act on that learning immediately.

Ultimately, personalization plus continuous learning allows you to maximize the value you receive from your digital experiences in a way that A/B testing simply was never intended to address.

CUTTING THROUGH THE DATA NOISE

Even in this book with "machine learning" in the title, we're not about to suggest that machines are taking over marketing and there will be no place for humans in the future. It's still up to humans, not machines, to develop and implement their own marketing and customer experience strategies. Machine learning can simply make

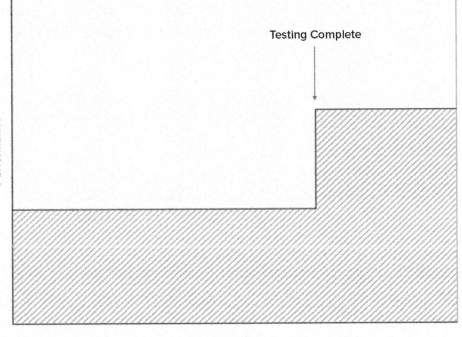

You don't receive the full benefit of an A/B test until the test is complete.

executing on those strategies possible.

But how do you come up with the ideas that fuel your marketing strategy? Often, those ideas come from a careful review of any data you can get your hands on. As a marketer, though, you have so much data available that it can be nearly impossible to discern which data you need to pay attention to. This is yet another place where machine learning and predictive analytics can help.

Think about all the data that exists within your company. That data can tell you how your marketing, and your business as a whole, is functioning. Yet the data exists in many different places and is often only accessible by certain members of the team. And even if you're bringing the critical pieces of customer information into a customer data platform, there will be many data sources you naturally won't include or won't regularly analyze. Data on your website performance, paid search campaigns, website promotions, traffic, overall email clickthrough rates, and more could still be sitting in multiple places across your organization.

Why is this relevant? With an enormous amount of data dispersed across the organization, it's not always easy to determine the true cause for any effect you see. Amazon once estimated that slowing its page load time by one second could cost it $1.6 billion in sales each year.[45] Realistically, how often are marketers paying close enough attention to notice something like that in a timely fashion? There's just too much data to analyze.

Machine learning can cut through the noise. It can make sense of all the signals in the data to help you identify patterns, opportunities or problems based on your key business metrics. You can use machine learning to analyze which campaign is providing the highest business impact, to recognize where opportunities exist in a marketing channel to help you plan future campaigns, or even to identify when a problem arises with existing personalization campaigns or general site performance. Machine learning can alert you to patterns and shifts in

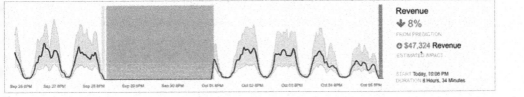

Revenue falls outside of predicted range; impact to business is predicted

those patterns so you can respond quickly and effectively.

How does this work? There are natural ebbs and flows for any business metric. But machine learning can quantify what the normal range tends to be with much more accuracy and ease than can humans reviewing reports alone. Then, predictive analytics can predict a range in which the value of the metric can be expected to fall on a given day. When a metric falls outside of that range, machines can call attention to the discrepancy and quantify the expected impact on business.

For example, a retailer could use machine learning and predictive analytics to evaluate typical inventory levels, taking into consideration seasonality, day of the week and general variation. The machine can recognize when shoppers are seeing more out-of-stock items than expected, helping the retailer to quickly identify the problem and to take immediate action. Or, a site focused on demand generation could use machine learning to analyze content downloads to identify when the number of leads generated is lower than predicted. The marketing team could then dig into that information to identify, for example, that an important link is broken (and to then correct it before too much damage is done).

This approach can save marketers time across all of their focus areas, including personalization. For example, machine learning could help a marketer determine which segments to target, which recommendations to fine-tune, which referring sources drive the best-quality traffic, or when a campaign is broken or no longer driving expected results. It remains, of course, the human's task to make decisions from there—including how to fix the problem, how to capitalize on the opportunity, and whether to implement a new campaign.

All marketers have ideas about what will provide a better experience. But it's not enough to implement what you think will work: you have to test your ideas to make sure you're right. Once an idea is tested, you can identify whether it is as successful as you hoped. If not, you can iterate until it works. And with the advent of machine learning, more and more of the testing and optimization process can be automated. Broadly speaking, testing allows you to understand the impact that personalization has on your business, so that those efforts do not become just another marketing tactic you can't quite measure.

CHAPTER 6 ENDNOTES

42. Scott Brinker, "Marketing Technology Landscape Supergraphic (2019): Martech 5000 (actually 7,040)," Chiefmartec.com, Apr 2019, https://chiefmartec. com/2019/04/marketing-technology-landscape-supergraphic-2019/.

43. Mariya Yao, "How AI can solve the top 3 pain points in marketing," Mar 2017, https://venturebeat.com/2017/03/21/ how-ai-can-solve-the-top-3-pain-points-in-marketing/.

44. Hubspot, Inc., "State of Inbound 2017," 2017, http://www.stateofinbound.com/.

45. Kit Eaton, "How One Second Could Cost Amazon $1.6 Billion in Sales," Mar 2012, https://www.fastcompany.com/1825005/ how-one-second-could-cost-amazon-16-billion-sales.

CHAPTER 7
PLANNING FOR PERSONALIZATION

Successfully delivering personalized experiences requires a different way of thinking than delivering non-personalized experiences. A marketing team putting personalization at the core of its strategy must shift from thinking about what *they would like to tell* their audiences, to what *each individual audience member wants to see*. When you implement personalization, instead of asking yourself, "What should we highlight on the homepage this month?" you would ask, "What does each of our key segments or personas need to learn from our homepage?" Instead of asking, "Which products and offers should we push today or this week?" you would ask, "What kinds of products and offers would individual visitors with different interests and needs prefer to see?" And instead of arranging your navigation or promoting your content in a way that makes the most sense to you and your team, you would consider how to present your content so that it will be the most relevant to each person on your site.

Essentially, personalization allows you to take the ultimate customer-centric marketing approach.

This is not a small shift that can happen overnight for many teams. Of course, as we discussed back in Chapter 5, it is certainly possible (and advisable) to dip your toe into the water first and implement a few basic campaigns to achieve some quick wins. However, in order to execute the type of one-to-one, cross-channel experiences that take full advantage of each person's preferences and intent with machine learning, you need to have a clear strategy.

Building a personalization program starts with getting the relevant stakeholders in your organization on the same page about the value and benefits of the initiative, defining a process and clarifying roles across the organization, developing a comprehensive strategy, and executing that strategy to achieve and measure success. In this chapter, we will address each of these areas in turn.

ORGANIZATIONAL DECISIONS TO MAKE

Larger organizations typically struggle more than their smaller counterparts when organizing for personalization. In small organizations, the number of people and teams involved in personalization is limited. Those organizations may have little to no established process—they can keep it informal and adapt as they learn more about what works and what doesn't. But when multiple teams need or want to be involved, an informal process will no longer cut it. In those situations, you should be clear about who in the organization is responsible for personalization in which situations and/or in which channels. Ideally, all of that information is written down and stored in an easily accessible place to hold everyone accountable and keep everyone on track.

We have assembled some questions you should consider as you get started. Not all questions will apply in all organizations, or the answers may be obvious depending on your situation or company size, but they are a good guide to use when kicking off the conversation.

MANAGEMENT
- How will you evaluate personalization success as an organization?
- Will you have a "personalization management office" (we'll define this later in the chapter) and how do you plan to have that office interact with your various divisions?
- Who will establish personalization strategy in each division?

- Who will assign personalization roles for staff in each division?
- How will management evaluate staff performance in these roles?
- How will you evaluate personalization success?
- What role would you like your technology and/or agency partners to play in personalization campaign strategy creation and execution?
- What channels will you personalize? Will you start with a single channel? How will you add others into your process when ready?

PLANNING

- How will you manage the ideation and prioritization of personalization campaigns?
- Who will establish and manage your personalization campaign calendar?
- How many campaigns do you expect to launch monthly across the organization and within each division?
- What are your busy periods? How will you manage high-traffic campaign development differently from other periods?
- How will your personalization team work with other teams to plan and execute your personalization campaign strategy?
- How will you share best practices and learnings across divisions?

TEAM ASSIGNMENT

- What groups and individuals are assigned to support personalization?
- What roles will each group and person play in your personalization strategy?
- What skill sets are required for the various roles?

EXPERIENCE DEVELOPMENT

• Who will decide the experiences to be developed?
• Who in your group will design your personalization experiences?
• Who will manage creative? Will this be a central function or located within each division?
• If more advanced coding is needed, will this be a central function or located within each division?
• Who will approve experience design work?

EXPERIENCE APPROVALS

• Who will test new experiences prior to launch?
• How will new experiences be approved prior to launch?
• Which kinds of experiences will need to be approved centrally and which within each divisions?
• When will experiences be launched?

OPTIMIZATION AND PERFORMANCE

• What key performance indicators are most important for your group and the larger organization?
• How will you analyze results (lift and impact)?
• How will you optimize experiences to continually improve results?

These questions may seem daunting, but don't forget that personalization can and should be an integral component of your customer experience and marketing efforts. If you think of it that way, rather than simply as just another one-off initiative your company is undertaking, you'll realize that taking these questions into consideration is extremely important.

We'll dive into more detail in several of these areas in the rest of this chapter.

ESTABLISH A PERSONALIZATION MANAGEMENT OFFICE

With so much to think about pertaining to personalization, larger organizations may consider establishing a "personalization management office" (PMO). As with a traditional project management office, a PMO allows organizations to build and scale a personalization program efficiently, forge accountability and ensure buy-in.

A PMO should be comprised of individuals from across different business groups and act as the main personalization strategy and solution or technical resource for the company, as well serve as the point of coordination across business divisions. Since personalization can touch multiple channels and teams, the PMO group can help make sure that all areas of the business are working toward the same goals—ultimately preventing headaches and greatly increasing the likelihood of success.

Each organization needs to figure out what the PMO should look like within its own context, but there are three broad steps you can take to establish one.

1. CREATE A PMO "CORE" TEAM

The first step in establishing a PMO is to identify the individuals who will be involved. Think of your personalization management office not as an entirely new business group, but rather a "task force" comprised of individuals from a variety of departments who act as a centralized personalization resource.

Who you include in the PMO depends on your business, but you should consider including key stakeholders from across the company—such as marketing (for all channels), analytics and operations. You should also consider nominating a strategic sponsor and program manager along with execution, analytics and creative team members. Do your best to keep from overloading the team, however, as having too many stakeholders involved can potentially make decision-making and execution slow.

Also, note that in smaller organizations, the PMO may simply be one or two individual contributors and an executive sponsor.

2. ESTABLISH YOUR PROCESS AND GOVERNANCE

Your PMO should be responsible for creating a roadmap for how your company develops and manages personalized experiences. Begin by examining what your current processes look like. How are customer experience initiatives currently rolled out in your organization? Who owns which aspects of that process? Once you identify how the customer experience is determined across channels and teams within the organization today, you can begin to work through how the process should shift to incorporate personalization.

As you work to incorporate personalization into your current workflows and business structure, select which individuals are responsible for different personalization tasks—both within the PMO and outside of it. Be explicit about who is involved with the personalization process and outline what each person's role is. Some will only be involved in the brainstorming process, with no additional input after that. Others will help make decisions about which campaigns to implement. Others still will be responsible for setting up and testing the campaigns. These may or may not be the same people who will actually publish campaigns. Establish these roles early.

When possible, set up role-based access control within your personalization platform. For example, create one set of users who can create campaigns, but not publish them. Create another set of users who can test campaigns. Then create a final set of those who can deploy campaigns into a published state. This structure will eliminate any confusion about roles and ensure that your campaigns are only deployed when the right members of your team review and sign off on them.

3. EXECUTE AND REPORT ON PROGRESS

The PMO should continue to check in on successful campaigns and determine which should be left alone, which can be improved, and which should be phased out. The definition of success will vary across companies, industries and channels.

The benefit of a PMO is that it can help aggregate learnings across teams and departments. If your company has multiple websites, you can test out a campaign on one site before rolling it out to others. A recommendation algorithm that was successful in an email could be rolled out to the website. Without a central group, those findings could be lost.

Finally, in addition to building out the organization's personalization strategy and processes, the PMO should be responsible for reporting results to management to ensure the program continues to garner buy-in and support.

DEFINE A PERSONALIZATION STRATEGY

While it is certainly possible to see impressive results without a personalization strategy simply by implementing campaigns here and there when you spot an opportunity, it is a good idea to develop a broader, long-term strategy, driven by a PMO. Even if it is simplistic, defining a strategy will help ensure you're achieving specific goals, prioritizing your ideas, measuring your success, and ultimately creating improved customer or prospect experiences.

The best place to start when developing your personalization strategy is with some initial research. We recommend three places to begin:

Your challenges and goals: Begin by thinking about the challenges you're facing and the goals you want to achieve with personalization. Increasing conversions, reducing bounce rate, improving ROI of a specific marketing tactic, increasing average order value, improving upsells and increasing retention are all common goals for marketers employing personalization. Push yourself to think beyond the challenge itself. Continue to ask yourself "Why?" whenever you identify a challenge or goal. For example, if you want to improve conversions (because everyone wants to improve conversions), ask yourself why that remains a goal. Why are you struggling with conversions today on your site? Why might one segment be converting better than another? You have to get to the root of a problem to address it.

Your data: If you are incessantly asking "Why?" during your strategy sessions, you will naturally turn to your data. What does your data say about your challenges? Where are the opportunities? Analyze the funnels on your site and identify the drop-off points. Find the low-hanging fruit, such as opportunities for lower exit rates for highly trafficked pages. After you identify your challenges and goals, form some hypotheses about why something is the way it is so you can begin to find answers within the data. We know that you have a lot of data available to you, so this stage can be quite overwhelming. But this process can help you uncover endless opportunities for improvement through personalization.

What is actually possible: At this point in the planning process, you and your team may have a lot of general ideas about how you want to leverage personalization. A concrete understanding of what is possible right now (both inside your organization as well as with existing technology) can help you refine those ideas. We hope that this book will give you a solid foundation, but you will probably want to supplement it with some conversations with vendors and additional research to understand what can be done with existing technology. There is a lot that can be accomplished today with current technology—far more than could be 20 years ago. But if your ideal personalization strategy involves tying online to offline via RFID chips implanted in each of your customers, you will find that you are currently out of luck. On the other hand, there is probably more available to you than you realize, so your strategy could end up even stronger than you originally expected.

Once you've begun digging into each of the above three areas, you should be ready to start fleshing out your personalization strategy. And as you document your processes, be sure to document your strategy as well. As you do so, consider including answers to each of these questions:

1. What are our goals?

Document the goals you identified earlier. You'll want to refer back to them when you start developing and prioritizing campaign ideas later on. Consider whether these ideas actually serve your goals. If not, are they worth doing? Or is it worth including additional goals you may have missed originally? Your documented goals can help you start that assessment.

2. How will we measure success?

Identify which metrics will determine whether you have reached your goals and document these metrics as a piece of your strategy. Without identifying metrics, you will not be able to quantify your success. Whatever the metrics are (e.g., conversion rate, click-through rate, AOV, revenues, retention rates, lifetime value, etc.), make sure you have a strong baseline and reasonable lift targets to help validate business impact.

3. Who are we targeting?

It is always a good idea to consider who you are targeting with your personalization efforts. In some cases, your targets will be audience segments, personas or industries across various channels. In other cases, you may want to use machine-learning algorithms to create unique experiences for each individual. With this approach, you will still want to document it, while considering whether you need different types of experiences or algorithms for different groups. Do you want to deliver different experiences to new versus returning visitors? What about customers versus prospects? These differences are important to note.

4. Where will we leverage personalization?

Consider which channels you currently use to communicate with customers, using the ones we discussed in Chapter 3 as a starting point. Which of those channels will be a part of your personalization strategy? Ideally, any channel you use to communicate with customers and prospects will be personalized in some way. Will you start with some channels before moving on to others? Prioritize your channels and think through your approach to each in advance.

5. What data sources do we need?

At this point, you already understand how important data is to a successful personalization strategy. But many organizations have data siloed across teams and systems, so it can be a lengthy process to bring it all together. You will want to start thinking early on about the data you need to reach your goals so you will have all the data sources you need to be successful.

Your data sources and your channels are inextricably linked, as well. Ideally, even channels you don't plan to include in your personalization strategy will still be involved via the data they collect. You should aim to bring the data from each channel into one system (such as your customer data platform) so it can be used to build out each person's unified customer profile. For example, even if you are planning to use personalization solely in your email campaigns and in-person channels, you should still aim to collect website and mobile app behaviors to help determine the most relevant experiences for each individual.

6. What content and creative do we need?

Much of the content you will need for personalization likely already exists in your organization. Still, it is important to think through this question early so you can start identifying any major gaps and planning on potential investments to address them. For example, if you want to create multiple homepage experiences for different audience segments, you will need to write new copy and design new images. Or, if you want to insert product recommendations on a page, you need to decide how many items to show and what "look and feel" to apply.

7. *What skills do we need?*

You will not get very far with your personalization strategy if you do not have people on your team or as part of your PMO with the requisite skills to accomplish your aims. But it is highly likely that you have such people on your staff now. They're doing web marketing, email marketing, product marketing, merchandising, and/or analytics already. If you use a personalization solution that doesn't require coding or the involvement of large teams, you will dramatically increase the chance that you can leverage the skills and talents of your existing staff. (We'll get more into the technology requirements in the next chapter.)

If you're starting small, you can probably rely on these existing staff members. But if you want to dive into a more advanced strategy right away—or if you've already tested personalization and want to do more—you may want to hire someone to lead your personalization efforts (full- or part-time). We predict that as more organizations make personalization a top priority, an increasing number of marketing teams will be looking to hire personalization specialists or directors of personalization to help them maximize the impact of these efforts.

While an ideal candidate would have a background in personalization campaigns, experience with other digital marketing campaigns (such as conversion optimization or demand generation, depending on your industry) could provide a sufficient foundation as well. Innovative email marketers, website/online marketers and marketing analytics specialists also make great candidates.

Once you have documented the answers to these questions—with input from all of your key stakeholders, of course—you should have a solid foundation for your personalization strategy.

IDENTIFYING THE RIGHT CAMPAIGNS

What is a campaign, precisely? Every personalization tactic you launch can be identified as a "campaign." For example, if you place "Complete the Look" recommendations on your product detail pages, you may call that a "Complete the Look Recommendations Campaign." Any homepage experience you use to target different industries or consumer segments you may call your "Homepage Hero Campaign." A triggered email sequence with relevant open-time email would be called a "Re-engagement Campaign." You would build and publish each of these campaigns in your personalization platform, which we will address in the next chapter.

When planning campaigns, the trouble is often deciding where to start. Even with the most robust strategy in place—and even after you have several successful campaigns under your belt—it is not always easy to select priorities among all of your campaign concepts. These steps may help:

1. IDENTIFY CAMPAIGNS

Begin by thinking about what you could do to address each of the main goals in your strategy. For example, to grow average order size, you may want to test recommendations on your cart page to pair with the items the shopper has in his cart. You could also suggest additional items the shopper can purchase that will allow him to qualify for free shipping. Or, to reduce bounce rate, you could create several different campaigns relevant to each visitor's referral source or location.

Continue to brainstorm tactics with your team to address all of your key goals and challenges. List out all of the tactics you can think of to address each goal, and indicate the channels and timing of these campaigns along with the metric(s) you'll need to measure their effectiveness.

2. PRIORITIZE CAMPAIGNS

Next, you'll want to establish a mechanism to help you prioritize your campaigns. We recommend something similar to the following image to weigh the anticipated impact against the expected level of difficulty to implement. This approach will help you determine which potential initiative will best advance your goals (without stretching your budget or team too thin). Particularly when you're just getting started with personalization, you should think about casting a wide net with your campaigns in terms of audience. Beginning with campaigns that will only reach ten people on your site is not the best use of your time. Comparing level of impact with expected level of difficulty can help you uncover that kind of high-labor, low-impact endeavor quickly.

If an idea is undemanding but high-impact, it's a no-brainer. Implement those campaigns immediately. Most likely, however, you'll end up with a chart slightly more complicated than that. Regardless, sketching out your concepts as above is a good way to begin to prioritize your initiatives.

3. TEST AND ITERATE

As with all of your marketing tactics, you should regularly test and iterate on your personalization campaigns. After you launch a new campaign, test it against a control to ensure that it provides a lift versus a non-personalized experience. Get into the habit of striving for continuous improvement—much like agile software

	IMPACT	DIFFICULTY
IDEA 1	HIGH	LOW
IDEA 2	MEDIUM	LOW
IDEA 3	LOW	MEDIUM

Sketching out campaign ideas can help you prioritize your initiatives.

development. Instead of analyzing, designing, coding and testing each new project in separate stages from start to finish, agile developers complete these steps concurrently—breaking each project into small chunks to rapidly deliver working software. This allows them to test early, discover problems quickly, and react fast.

As a marketer focusing on personalizing your entire customer, shopper or prospect experience, you can operate in a similar way. That means you shouldn't just develop one campaign at a time and wait to see if it works. Instead, you must develop a process where you are always evaluating and refining current campaigns, testing new ones, and removing those that don't work or that have become outdated.

Think back to the goals you defined. It is possible that one of those goals can be considered "completed" after a certain time. But it is more likely that there is no real "finish line." Specific metrics such as conversion rate or engagement can always be gradually improved, and such small improvements ultimately compound into larger ones that can have a sizable impact on your bottom line. Even more abstract goals such as "improve customer experience" can always be improved upon, as technology and customer expectations are continually evolving.

Ultimately, personalization is not a single end to a single problem. It is an ongoing process, and constant iteration is the key to ensuring that process keeps moving forward.

Of course, as a marketer, you are being pulled in many different directions at once. It is not always easy to find the time for continuous iteration. You can start by blocking out some time each week or setting a regular meeting with your PMO to evaluate your campaigns. You should continuously be adding, refining and discarding campaigns—as well as evaluating the effectiveness of your backbone campaigns. More on these aims:

Add new campaigns: You should always be trying new tactics as you develop new content, products, features and more. Are you successfully engaging the right audiences through the right channels? Do your messaging and imagery across channels resonate with these audiences? Is there a new segment your company wants to better engage and convert? How can you make your cross-channel communication even more one-to-one? These are the questions that you should be asking as you think about and prioritize new campaign ideas and as you decide when and which campaigns to add. There is no universal recommendation on how many campaigns you should implement or how frequently you should launch them. But if you are not testing new campaigns, your program will certainly stagnate.

Refine a few campaigns: Take a look at what you launched last week, last month and last year. Are all the campaigns still working? Could they work better if they were improved? Could you optimize your rules or algorithms or incorporate new creative? Don't just set a campaign and forget it: test and tweak it until you see improvement—and come back to it now and then to ensure it still works.

Discard a few campaigns: What worked in the past might not work now. Maybe that campaign that you tweaked to perfection several months ago finally ran its course. If you're not seeing any gain from a campaign and all your adjustments aren't helping, you should let it go. Also consider that messaging can become outdated, so you need to monitor your campaigns to ensure they're on-message and on-brand. Toss, replace or update them once they're not.

Evaluate your backbone campaigns: Keep in mind that constant iteration doesn't mean that you always need to be throwing out or refining all of your campaigns. Many marketers have "backbone campaigns" that they create, iterate on one or twice, and then let run continuously. These campaigns often dependably drive results while you are developing other ideas. You need to find the right mix that works for you and your organization. But don't forget to evaluate these campaigns regularly to make sure they're still working.

Campaigns are challenging to prioritize and update, but their impact is indisputable. Use the above tips to develop your own repeatable process that drives a continuously improved experience for your visitors and customers.

CONVINCING YOUR ORGANIZATION TO INVEST IN PERSONALIZATION

Before we conclude, let's take a brief step back. This chapter has explored how to establish the processes and strategy to effectively deliver personalization in your organization. But what if you can't get your organization to agree to prioritizing personalization in the first place?

Depending on your role in your organization, you could be facing objections from executive leadership, IT or other members of the marketing team, or all of the above. The main objections we hear from those in leadership positions include:

I don't see the value.

As with all new investments, you may need to convince senior leadership of the value of personalization. In many cases, though, this will not be necessary. Personalization is a common buzzword in the world of marketing, and many leaders are already familiar enough with it to understand the value it can bring to their customers and their organization.

But if it is necessary, we hope that after getting this far in the book you are fully versed in the benefits of personalization and are ready to share some of that knowledge with your leadership team. It also helps to think about the main use cases you have in mind for personalization in your own channels and to share those ideas with your leadership team. Think about the impact you expect those initiatives will achieve, and quantify it for the team. If you think that you could increase your conversion rate, for example, by how much do you expect it to increase? What does that mean for your bottom line? For most marketers we have spoken to, even modest increases in conversion rate, retention, sign-up, upsells, page views, and average order value, etc., can have a substantial impact. Be sure to take advantage of tools available to compute the ROI of investments in personalization.

Additionally, the competitive advantage can't be ignored. Given the history and growth of one-to-one communication over the last 20 years, it's clear that as a society we're headed toward more personalization, not less. The ability to provide personalized experiences is often a competitive advantage—for now. In the future, a personalized approach will be critical to any business' success. Explaining to your leadership team that it is important to get started now will make a difference.

We don't have the budget.

No matter how you go about delivering personalization, you will require a budget. The tactics you take will vary dramatically depending on your organization. The best advice we can give is that, in addition to quantifying the expected impact to your KPIs, you should do the math to identify the ROI you would receive. That means determining how much you plan to spend on personalization in a year and weighing that against the expected (positive) impact to your business. We have found that the right technology can pay for itself in spades with the improvements gained.

There aren't enough resources to manage it.

Similar to the budgetary concern, leadership may object that the team does not have the bandwidth to manage a personalization effort. If new team members and skills development are not a near-term option, it could help to go in the "small wins" direction—particularly if you have a small team. We have found that it does not take much time (sometimes even just an hour or two a week) to plan and execute a few quick and easy campaigns that generate nice lifts in conversion rate, engagement, average order size, email capture rate and beyond. If leadership sees the value in personalization and is willing to allocate the budget, but is worried about these efforts taking too much time from the team, starting small and growing your investment from there could lead to success.

Even once your leadership is on board (or if you are in leadership yourself), you may still need to manage objections from other members of your marketing team. These are the few we hear most often:

I'm already overwhelmed; this will take up too much of my time.

A common complaint from small marketing teams—often stretched too thin—is that they do not need another tactic to manage. This is a fair complaint, but it is up to you to convey the value that personalization can bring, explain that the benefits will outweigh the cost of their time, and determine the initiative's priority relative to others.

Just like with senior leadership, give some thought to some of the main use cases you have in mind for personalization and consider the impact you would see from increasing your KPIs. Many team members will be excited by those use cases if they improve the end experience for customers or prospective customers. And if they are not excited by the improved experience alone, they may be swayed by the expected lifts—particularly if the team's performance is measured against those KPIs.

If this objection is a concern for you as well, make sure you invest in a technology that is easy to use—one that your team will not find cumbersome or tedious to use or that does not need too much training to learn. The prospect of learning a new, strategic technology to add to their resumes is often exciting for team members as well.

We're going through a redesign, and we don't have a finished product to work with.

Many marketers use a redesign of their websites, mobile or web apps as an excuse to avoid personalization, claiming that it isn't a good time. For some situations, that may be true. But in many cases, it is a good idea to incorporate personalization into your newly designed site or app from the beginning. You are often able to find even more uses for personalization when you're planning to transform the baseline experience.

For example, any area of your site that you plan to be static could in fact have multiple versions targeted to different segments. You could even determine where all of your product and/or content recommendations will be placed and start testing different algorithms. At a minimum, you and your team might want to begin thinking about how to leverage personalization early.

We don't have enough existing content for personalization.

Many content-based teams are nervous that they will have to multiply the amount of content they currently have by the number of personas they want to target. But the reality is that most sites already have plenty of content that is written for different personas or stages of the funnel. That content just isn't always targeted effectively.

Personalization can be used to bring the relevant content to the forefront for each visitor on your site. For example, rather than relying on the visitor to navigate to your resources page and select the right eBook, you can recommend that content on any page of your site and when it's most appropriate for each visitor.

Of course, implementing personalization can help you identify any content gaps you may have. But those gaps might not be essential to fill before getting started with personalization.

In this chapter, we have discussed the issues of making important organizational decisions relevant to personalization, establishing a personalization management office, developing a personalization strategy, executing your personalization program, keeping the program running smoothly and addressing objections to personalization.

Of course, no personalization strategy is complete without the right technology to appropriately act on data to provide the most relevant experiences in the moment. That's the focus of the next chapter.

CHAPTER 8

FINDING THE RIGHT TECH FOR THE JOB

In the last chapter, we covered how to get started with personalization in your organization. But before you can get very far, you need the right technology. As the foundation of your personalization program, it is essential that your technology has the ability to collect, analyze and act on data in real time to deliver a personalized experience. And for one-to-one personalization, the technology must incorporate machine-learning capabilities, be highly sophisticated, and garner a considerable level of trust from the business user.

By adopting machine learning, you are entrusting technology to manage pieces of your marketing and customer experience delivery. Relinquishing control can be disconcerting to many. How do you know what the end result looks like for your visitors, users, shoppers and customers if each person's experience is different? How can you guarantee the experiences will be good?

Most marketers we've spoken with feel more comfortable with machine learning when they have control over the experiences the machine delivers. Yet many solutions operate as a "black box": they provide dynamic experiences (primarily in the form of recommendations), but not much insight into how those experiences are determined. And if they give you no insight into how they are picking experiences, then they certainly don't give you much insight into how well they are performing or how they could be improved.

In this chapter, we'll review the main requirements of the technology needed to support one-to-one personalization. We'll also provide tips on how to spot black boxes and other potential red flags with vendors.

PERSONALIZATION AND CUSTOMER DATA PLATFORMS

Throughout this book, we've made references to different technologies as your "personalization engine," "personalization platform" or "customer data platform." So you may be thinking, which of these do I need for personalization? Can one-to-one personalization be executed with just one solution? Or does it require an ecosystem of solutions working together?

Unfortunately, the answer is "it depends."

No single solution on the market today offers the same feature set, nor do they all refer to themselves by the same name or category. You need to fully outline your company's needs in the short and long term and compare that against the functionality offered in the market to find the solution(s) that best meet your current and future needs. However, we do have some recommendations for how to think about your tech stack.

Data is the foundation of any good personalized experience—so first, you must collect information about a person. Then, you can decide which experience is the most relevant based on that information. With that in mind, you can think about your technology as serving two main purposes: insight and engagement.

In this context, a **system of insight** aggregates customer/prospect data and enables analysis of that data.

A **system of engagement** delivers experiences to customers/prospects in one or more channels and enables measurement of the outcome.

Your tech stack must address both insight and engagement. Organizations sometimes break up their purchasing process for these capabilities into two parts. They may decide to purchase a solution that serves as a system of insight initially, while they decide to purchase or connect it to system(s) of engagement six to nine months later after they have made progress with the first solution. This approach is primarily driven by the increasing attention on customer data platforms (CDPs)—which, as you'll remember from earlier in the book, serve as a central location for customer data in an organization. In other words, a CDP is a system of insight.

There are two main problems with separating CDP and personalization functionality into different systems.

1. LIMITATIONS OF SEGMENTS

Systems of insight are primarily designed to evaluate and identify audience segments and then pass the data about segment membership to a separate system of engagement. Segment data is undoubtedly valuable in many situations (we've described a number of segment-driven experiences in this book), but when the system of insight can only pass segment-level data to another system for engagement, you do not have the option to deliver one-to-one experiences.

As a result, your only option to approximate one-to-one personalization is to create more and more segments and map those segments to specific campaigns. In effect, you will be forced to decide between increased relevance and increased complexity because, as you will recall from Chapter 2, growing your number of segments to get closer to one-to-one personalization becomes increasingly complex and difficult to manage.

2. SUBOPTIMAL ARCHITECTURE

Having two platforms—a CDP and a separate personalization platform—effectively creates a technology environment with two "brains." Obviously, systems of insight are a type of advanced, centralized brain full of customer data that generates insights from that data. In reality, though, systems of engagement must also act as a brain. They need to leverage machine learning to sift through the vast amount of customer data and make the best decision about which experience, content, promotion, message or recommendation to deliver to each individual at any given moment in each channel.

It doesn't make sense to have all of your customer data live in both of these systems, nor does it make sense to feed your system of engagement limited data from the system of insight to make a decision about which experience to deliver.

EXAMPLE

The idea that one solution can provide a dramatically better experience than two can be difficult to conceptualize. Let's explore an example to help illuminate this point. In this example, we'll look at two different customers of a retail company, Susan Jones and Susan Smith. A snapshot of each Susan's hypothetical profile data appears on the opposite page. The data reflects that they each have exhibited different behaviors and have different preferences.

Let's say, as the retailer in this example, you want to engage both Susans with an email campaign to remind them that they have loyalty points to spend. You might begin by putting both of them into a segment of customers who have outstanding loyalty points in your system of insight, push that segment to one of your systems of engagement (such as your ESP), and use the ESP to send an email campaign to the segment. In other words, each Susan will receive the same exact email.

This campaign may have some impact, but it is not particularly relevant to each person, and it is a far cry from one-to-one person-

Each "Susan" has a distinct customer profile with different purchase behavior, patterns and preferences.

alization.

To personalize further, you might decide to make *additional* segments for a few of your product categories and assign each Susan to a segment based on her category affinity. If you mapped each narrower segment to a specific campaign in your ESP, each Susan would receive an email relevant to her favorite category that also reminds her of the loyalty points.

This approach may not sound like an unmanageable number of segments, but it can quickly get out of control as you set up each segment in your CDP and then map those segments to a large number of campaigns in your ESP.

For instance, you need to make a "have outstanding loyalty points" segment for every major product category (e.g., seasonal furniture + have outstanding loyalty points; household goods + have outstanding loyalty points, etc.) and map it to a matching campaign in your ESP. But you likely won't have just one campaign. You will also want to engage customers who are not in the loyalty program, who are active loyalty members, who are likely to churn, etc. More still, you may want to differentiate among customers not just by category interest and loyalty status, but also by their tendency to respond to offers (and what type of offer they respond to).

With such added complexity, you must add more and more segments and build more and more experiences.

Keep in mind that this example isn't an individually relevant experience determined by machine learning—it's a marketer-defined experience driven by rules and segments. An individually relevant email would include a banner chosen for each person regardless of which segment they belong to, as well as recommendations for products they have recently shopped or those they might be interested in based on their preferences. That simply can't be achieved with segments alone.

In addition, this is just one example on one channel, so you can

Susan Jones receives the email on the left because she's part of a segment of people who have outstanding loyalty points and a known preference for seasonal furniture. Susan Smith receives the email on the right because she's part of a segment of people who have outstanding loyalty points and a known preference for household goods.

see how the problem expands exponentially with different campaigns across channels. As a result, most companies end up curbing their ambitions and instead settle for some group-level relevance.

SO WHAT DOES ALL THIS MEAN?

What are we trying to say with this long example about segments and emails? When most standalone CDPs on the market, acting as systems of insight, pass data to systems of engagement, they do so at the segment level only. This can work in some instances, such as when you just want to send the same email to members of a loyalty program, as we explored in the beginning of the previous example. But if you want to send an email, display a web experience, target an ad, etc. containing the most relevant content to an individual, you need your system of engagement to be able to access individual-level data.

Thus, our recommendation is to select your system of insight and your system of engagement at the same time so you're thinking about the end-to-end process. **You will likely find that combining insight and engagement functionality into one single solution is the best approach.**

One caveat here: Given the number of channels you will likely include in your personalization program, it is not realistic to assume that you will be able to find activation capabilities for all of them in one system of engagement. But the overall concept still applies: you want to limit the number of solutions you include in your personalization program to avoid unnecessary complexities and shortcomings.

HIGH-LEVEL TECHNOLOGY REQUIREMENTS FOR PERSONALIZATION

No matter which technologies you decide to incorporate into your tech stack, you'll need a few must-have features for one-to-one personalization. Keep in mind, these are critical aspects of an effective solution, not an exhaustive list. Use this list as a starting point for thinking about your personalization program requirements.

A SINGLE, ACTIONABLE PROFILE FOR EVERY SINGLE PERSON

By this point, it should be abundantly clear that it's impossible to deliver an experience that is unique and relevant to an individual if you don't have a comprehensive understanding of that individual. Imagine several different people observing a shopper in a physical store at different times. Each would observe distinct actions, so if they don't share their observations, they will each have a very different view of his preferences and intent.

In the digital world, successful personalization requires that all of your in-depth behavioral data from across channels be captured, synchronized with external attribute data, and brought together into a single profile for each visitor, customer and account. However, a single profile is not easy to deliver and hard to find among vendors. Many martech vendors will appear to provide a complete platform that offers capabilities across the full personalization spectrum, but merging data sources is either impossible with their existing tools or very complex and time-consuming.

Look for solutions with clear features for resolving identities, prioritizing identifiers, aggregating individual-level data, stitching profiles, and more. This functionality provides the foundation for delivering a single, actionable profile for each person.

ROBUST INTEGRATIONS WITH OTHER SYSTEMS

Your personalization technology should not introduce another silo into your organization. To create that single profile for each individual, you need to be able to bring data in from other sources seamlessly. And you need to be able to push data out to trigger actions or keep other systems up-to-date. With martech stacks becoming more and more complicated, this is an area you can't ignore in your search for personalization technology.

Look for systems with robust sets of integration capabilities including out-of-the-box integrations, robust documented APIs, ETL capabilities, and a generally extensible integration framework that allow your developers to easily connect the platform to outside systems.

THE ABILITY TO UNDERSTAND BUSINESS CONTEXT

Every business is different, and each business's products and content are unique, with their own unique attributes. For example, a jeweler cares about the cut and carat of its diamonds, while a fashion retailer cares about brands and colors of its clothing and accessories. A content publisher may care about the author of its articles, while a B2B company cares about the keywords in its blog articles.

Your business is not about pages or events; it is centered around products and content. If your personalization technology can only identify that a jewelry shopper viewed three product pages, for example, but it can't understand cut and carat, it won't be able to recognize that the shopper is interested in princess-cut diamonds over 1.00 carat in size. That information is imperative to a jeweler.

Your personalization technology must be able to understand business context so you can know not just which pages a person has visited, but what their behaviors and interactions with your products and content actually tell you about who that person is and what her interests and affinities are.

THE ABILITY TO CREATE SEGMENTS AND LEVERAGE MACHINE LEARNING

Good data gives you a strong understanding of your customers, but after you have that understanding, you need to be able to act on it.

As we have already discussed, personalized experiences are typically delivered via rules (at the segment level) and machine-learning algorithms (at the individual level). Your personalization technology must give you the flexibility to build as many segments and rules as you need, as well as the visibility and flexibility to pick and modify algorithms to deliver the types of personalized experiences you envision.

THE ABILITY TO ACT ON ANY AND ALL DATA IN REAL TIME

We tend to be forgiving when anyone says that something is available in "real time." We often take that to mean "quickly" or "soon" rather than the phrase's real definition: "the actual time during which a process takes place or an event occurs."[46]

In terms of personalization, "real time" refers to the *actual moment that someone is interacting with a company*. When we say that the data should be used to deliver a personalized experience in real time, we mean it should be delivered the *actual moment* a person is interacting with the company, regardless of the channel—based on her behavior in real time. All aspects of every visitor's complete history must be combined with everything she is doing in the moment, and everything you've learned about her from all relevant sources, to deliver a personalized experience across channels—in a matter of milliseconds.

The term is used liberally in many vendors' marketing messages—and isn't always meant in its full sense—but true real-time is absolutely essential to delivering relevant experiences that leverage a person's in-the-moment, not past, intent.

THE ABILITY TO MANAGE THE TECHNOLOGY WITHOUT THE NEED FOR IT OR ENGINEERING INVOLVEMENT

If you are a marketer, you've probably experienced the pain that results from relying on other teams in your organization to accomplish your marketing goals. Whether you need assistance from engineering, IT, customer success or sales, it can be frustrating when other teams—weighted down with their own priorities—fail to put your initiatives at the top of the list. When it comes to something as important as the customer experience, you don't want to wholly rely on others. So what can you do?

With the right technology, you and your team should be able to launch, measure and adjust personalization campaigns quickly and easily on your own, without intervention. Yet the platform needs to be comprehensive enough to address all of your complex multi-tactic, cross-channel demands. With some vendors, a platform like this just does not exist.

That said, if your IT and engineering teams are essential marketing partners, the right platform should provide the reporting, developer tools, interfaces and APIs to enable these teams to accomplish their goals as well. Make sure you understand everyone's needs to determine whether prospective personalization solution vendors can meet them.

ACCURATE ATTRIBUTION ANALYSIS

As we described in Chapters 6 and 7, testing, analytics and attribution analysis are critical components of any personalization campaign. Without the ability to test, you cannot know if your campaigns are successful or if there is anything you can do to improve your approach. You need built-in testing and attribution analysis to iterate rapidly and ensure your experiences and algorithms deliver the best results possible.

Some solutions are not transparent when it comes to attribution analysis. Some vendors will provide reporting on campaign results but not enable customers to run or manage those reports themselves. And many will boldly claim that their "black box" solutions have made you hundreds of thousands or even millions in incremental revenue—taking credit for growth that may have occurred anyway. When selecting a personalization solution, make sure that you have the ability to compare the results of every campaign against control and that the solution utilizes sound statistical science for accurate and defensible attribution analysis.

HOW TO EVALUATE CDP AND PERSONALIZATION VENDORS

When evaluating any new vendor solution, it can be a challenge to sort out real strengths from exaggerated claims. The terms used throughout this book—"one-to-one," "real-time," "intent," "attribution," "integrated"—are common buzzwords in the industry. They're so frequently used that they can lose their meaning. Additionally, because virtually every email platform, CMS vendor, large technology company and small martech vendor has realized the critical importance of personalization and customer data, almost every such provider claims to be a personalization and/or customer data platform—whether they truly are or not.

It is critical, therefore, to ask the right questions. The capability to implement one-to-one personalization is out there; it's just a matter of finding the right technology for your needs. These questions should help you unravel and evaluate a potential vendor's sales pitch.

Does your solution allow for one-to-one personalization? If so, can I see a single unified customer profile?

If one-to-one personalization is important to you (and we assume it is if you're reading this book), then you need to make sure that each personalization vendor you consider can help provide true one-to-one experiences. Recall how in the '90s, BroadVision positioned its product as "One-to-One" when it only supported simple rule-based communication to broad segments. Many vendors today remain about as vague about what their "one-to-one" solutions provide. Some only offer recommendations based on what other visitors have viewed; others merely enable you to create rules or pass data out to other systems to deliver personalized experiences to segments. These types of experiences are valuable, of course, but they're not the unique experiences delivered at the individual level that a modern personalization program should support.

To ensure that personalization can be delivered at the individual level, ask to see a vendor's single, unified customer profile—the individual profile that stores all of the data on an individual person or, for B2B needs, on an individual account. If a vendor cannot produce one, or if it can only take in segment data from another system, it cannot effectively deliver on its one-to-one claims.

What channels do you support? Are all channels supported by the same, unified platform and driven by the same, unified customer profile?

The main channels we've identified are website, web app, mobile web, mobile app, email, search, digital advertising, social, direct mail and human. Make sure you determine which channels you want to personalize and then ensure that those channels are fully supported by the vendor. A vendor's solution should be equipped to collect in-depth data from your selected channels, take in data from other systems, and deliver personalized experiences through these channels.

It is also worthwhile to ascertain how support for each channel was built into the vendor's solution. Did the vendor natively build the capabilities or gain them through acquisitions? If the latter, dig into how well the various acquired solutions work together. If they do not integrate seamlessly, there could be a lag when data is passed from one solution to another. Also, determine whether all cross-channel functionality can be managed from one platform and whether all data from each channel appears in the same unified customer profile. If not, executing cross-channel personalization—and real-time personalization especially—might be difficult or impossible.

What data sources do you support and how easily can they be integrated?

Think in advance about what data sources you plan to integrate and utilize for your personalization efforts. Do you have data in your CRM, email/marketing automation platform, data warehouses, or other places that you need in order to create a complete picture of each user (whether that person is known or anonymous)? If so, make sure that the data can be leveraged and integrated via out-of-the-box capabilities or robust APIs. You don't want to sacrifice data that could be valuable for personalization.

Can the platform pass data and trigger actions to other systems?

Whether you're looking for a standalone CDP, a standalone personalization platform, or a combination of the two, it won't be the only system in your marketing tech stack. It should be equipped to pass data it collects or processes to any marketing technology you use, in batch or in real time.

Triggered actions are an advanced capability that allow one

system to immediately inform, update or direct other systems via workflows set up by business users. For example, the platform could trigger a task in the CRM to follow up with a target prospect account that just spent quality time on key pages of your site, or an automated customer service call from a call center to a customer who just made a high-value purchase, or an email to a shopper about items left in his cart.

How do you define "real time"?

The definition of "real time" varies across vendors. Make sure that any prospective vendor's understanding of the term aligns with your own. When you ask a vendor to define it, the answer should be unequivocal: the solution considers all data for each visitor from the current and all past sessions, applies any and all personalization logic, renders the personalized experience, and supports reporting and analysis of that experience—all in milliseconds. Any answer that involves a delay of any kind in this end-to-end process is not, in fact, "real time."

What behavioral data do you collect?

As we outlined in Chapter 4, combining deep behavioral data with contextual data is essential for creating relevant experiences across channels. Without it, you cannot truly understand the affinities and in-the-moment intent of each person. Still, most vendors, if they are tracking data, only track page visits and clicks.

Ask about the behavioral data each vendor collects to understand if they are really measuring engagement (including time spent, mouse movement, scrolling, hovering and inactivity) as well as page-level metadata (such as categories, tags, brands, colors and keywords). If they are not, you risk running personalization campaigns with an incomplete understanding or your visitors and customers.

How do you determine an individual's affinities and in-the-moment intent?

An effective and maximally relevant one-to-one experience requires knowing what a person likes and what he is looking for right now. Getting to that level of understanding requires machine learning to analyze large data sets to garner insights. If a vendor is not able to answer how these insights are gleaned with its solution, you should be cautious about trusting the accuracy of the resulting personalization.

What does machine learning look like in your platform?

Given the importance of machine learning for one-to-one personalization, you need to understand a vendor's machine-learning capabilities from the beginning. Does the vendor's platform allow you to create smarter segments with automatic clustering (as described in Chapter 2)? Is it capable of applying machine learning to do affinity modeling to determine a person's true preferences and intent, and predictive modeling to determine a person's future actions (as explained in Chapter 4)? Can the vendor's platform use machine learning for alerting, troubleshooting, and problem and opportunity identification (as described in Chapter 6)? Most importantly, can you customize your machine-learning algorithms to deliver one-to-one communication across channels? And can you leverage these algorithms to deliver more than just product or content recommendations, but also brands, categories, promotions, search results, sorted lists and dynamic navigation?

If any of these areas are important to your personalization strategy, be sure to select a vendor that will help you execute them.

What does attribution reporting look like within your solution?

You must be allowed to control your own analytics to dive as deep into the data as you wish. You should ask any vendor how their analytics and attribution capabilities work. Does the solution allow you to compare all campaign performance against a control? How is statistical significance determined? Can you calculate the impact of your campaigns on multiple metrics so you can understand site-wide impact? Are you able to customize the attribution window to uncover the impact during different time periods? If you can't easily determine the answers to these questions, you might be dealing with a "black box" solution.

How do you use your own product for digital marketing?

If you notice a vendor has been a bit vague in some of their responses, try this question. While not an essential factor in the decision, any vendor should probably be using its own product to deliver personalized experiences in its own marketing channels. After all, you wouldn't trust a chef who doesn't eat her own cooking, would you? Even if you're a B2C company, you can still learn a lot from how a personalization technology vendor leverages its own product. At the very least, a vendor should be prepared to cite specific and effective examples of personalization on their site. A great vendor should give you a comprehensive demo of personalization in action across channels, showing you how relevant and engaging experiences are delivered at the one-to-one level—in real time—and explaining what business strategies each personalization campaign supports.

If a vendor can't offer these examples and demonstrations, that might be an indication that the product does not meet some of the criteria we have laid out in this book. It could also mean that the solution is difficult or cumbersome to use—and even the company's own marketing team might not be able to leverage it.

BUILD VERSUS BUY

Throughout the chapter, we've described the requirements of personalization and customer data technology with the assumption that you'll be using a third-party vendor (i.e., that you will purchase the technology instead of building it yourself). As with any new initiative, marketers must decide whether to build or buy the technology that will drive it. For many marketers, particularly those with limited development resources, the decision to purchase is easily reached. For others, it requires more analysis.

Businesses tend to (rightly) view personalization as a potential competitive differentiator—one that they would like to keep closely guarded. As a result, some explore the possibility of building their own technology solution. They don't want their competitors to know how their personalized experiences are being generated and what goes into them. If you are considering this approach, we encourage you to ask yourself these questions:

- Will building personalization or customer data software distract from your core business?
- Can you develop a single unified profile for each individual, and take in data from multiple sources to build out those profiles?
- Can you develop all you need for cross-channel personalization, as outlined in this book?
- Do you have data scientists to develop the machine-learning algorithms and predictive intelligence necessary for one-to-one personalization?
- Can you seamlessly integrate what you build into your existing tech stack?
- Can you develop a solution that is easy for marketers and other business people to use?

- Can you launch the solution in a timely fashion and keep up with future needs?
- Are you prepared to dedicate resources to maintain the solution?
- Can you keep up with personalization and CDP best practices, strategies and tactics?
- How does the cost of building and maintaining your company's own solution compare to that of a third-party solution?

If you build your own personalization solution, you will have control over the features it includes, how it works, and what the user interface looks like. Some organizations opt to take this route, particularly when they believe it will give them a competitive advantage.

But realistically, if you choose to buy your personalization technology, you do not need to worry about losing your competitive advantage. Your technology will only be as good as the work that you put into it. Even if you and your major competitors all use the same solution, you will not be using the same customized algorithms, designing the same campaigns, or iterating on existing experiences in the same way.

———

Selecting the best technology for your personalization plan is essential. You may have a lot of ideas about how you would like to use personalization as part of your marketing strategy, but those ideas will not get off the ground if you don't have the technology to support them. Picking vendors is not a decision you should take lightly.

That said, choosing a personalization solution vendor does not need to be overwhelming. As long as you know what to look for, you will be able to separate fact from fiction, determine what's real-time versus "next-time" personalization, and distinguish a comprehensive customer data platform that allows you to deliver individualized experiences from a CDP that only allows for segment-based communication.

Here's a quick recap of the top pitfalls to watch out for when evaluating vendors:

- When data can only be collected from, and experiences only be delivered to, one or a limited number of channels

- Instances where "real time" doesn't mean "the actual moment when an event or process occurs"

- When "one-to-one personalization" does not factor in an accurate understanding of an individual's affinities or in-the-moment intent

- CDPs that *collect* data at the individual level, but can only *act on* data at the segment level

- Insufficient testing and attribution capabilities, or math that does not add up

- Cumbersome user interfaces, or any platform that cannot be operated by a non-technical team

- Any over-reliance on buzzwords without the ability to fully explain what they mean

- A suite that has been pieced together through poorly integrated acquisitions

CHAPTER 8 ENDNOTE

46. real time. Dictionary.com. Dictionary.com Unabridged. Random House, Inc., http://www.dictionary.com/browse/real-time?s=t.

CHAPTER 9
THE FUTURE OF PERSONALIZATION

When Peppers and Rogers wrote *The One-to-One Future* in 1994, they described how the Information Revolution was about to fundamentally change the way businesses interacted with customers. They hypothesized that:

> *The 1:1 marketing paradigm will put customers first, and the most successful marketers will be those that build the deepest, most trusting relationships with their individual customers. Economies of scope will enable small competitors to defeat large ones, at least in the share-of-customer battle for specific, individual customers.*[47]

We can probably all agree that their prediction has become a reality. In the last few years, companies have disrupted industries by putting customers first, delivering personalized experiences, and creating truly innovative solutions. One such example is Netflix. As of this book's publication, Netflix has nearly 150 million subscribers worldwide and is continuing to expand its user base globally. It added 9.6 million new subscribers in the first quarter of 2019 alone.[48] Netflix can be credited with forever altering consumer expectations about content consumption, bringing the concept of "binge-watching" mainstream.

As a streaming video platform, Netflix faces stiff competition from other streaming video providers, cable providers, and all other sources of entertainment. Netflix differentiates against all of this competition by providing a personalized customer experience. Chris

Jaffe, VP of Product Innovation, has said:

> *We have to make customers happy and that's the single guiding light. As we think about customers, we think about how they are spending their time. The biggest challenge for Netflix is: if you're tired and it's the end of the day, you could read a book or a magazine, you could go on Facebook, watch linear TV, or watch Netflix. We want to make Netflix so engaging you keep choosing it.*[49]

Rather than simply depending on users to search for specific content or listing all available content in alphabetical order, Netflix offers specific recommendations across its platform to each user based on his or her individual preferences. This level of personalization starts with a deep understanding of its users and their preferences. Recommendations are generated using a collaborative filtering algorithm, which shows users content they are most likely to be interested in based on their individual viewing behavior and how that behavior compares to viewers with similar behaviors. The algorithm also incorporates variations to show users that there are other genres available that they may not have been exposed to before. The algorithm learns more about the users from how they interact with those variants—whether they engage with them or not—to determine viewers' interest in those genres (this aspect of machine learning is called "self-learning"). Additionally, Netflix's algorithmically generated search results consider an individual's preferences and the popularity of the content. Finally, Netflix is always testing the user interface and the functionality of its platform to drive continued improvements to the overall experience.[50]

Personalization stories like Netflix's make clear that Peppers and Rogers' vision is now possible. Its approach has enabled the company to capture the mindshare and wallet share of nearly 150 million viewers and to compete with and win over big cable companies. Netflix's story also encapsulates all the personalization concepts we have described in this book. From using data to understand each individual user, to delivering one-to-one personalization through machine learning, to continued testing and iteration, Netflix is leveraging personalization at a remarkable level.

Today, most marketers are not delivering personalization to the degree that Netflix is, nor are they leveraging everything we have described in this book. That is to be expected. There are always early adopters of newer technologies, and there are always marketers that push boundaries and break the mold. For many marketers, the future involves transitioning to a strategy that puts personalization at the center of their business strategies (not just their marketing strategies) and implementing the types of personalization we have described in this book. The technologies to accomplish true personalization exist, but the transition will take some time. Marketers who are not yet personalizing any of their efforts certainly need to launch these initiatives soon, however—or they will risk irrelevance.

But beyond the clear and knowable future—and what we have outlined in this book—here are a few predictions about how personalization will evolve over the next years and decades.

THE FUTURE OF B2C

There are a few trends facing B2C marketing that will guide personalization in the future. First, ask any B2C marketer and he or she will tell you that competition for consumer attention is fierce. The internet has lowered the barriers to reaching an audience: smaller businesses can easily reach their target consumers with fewer resources than larger companies, and anyone can be a content creator with their own blog, a video producer with their own channel on YouTube, or a retailer with their own shop on Etsy. As a result, B2C companies are increasingly finding that they need to differentiate based on their customer experiences, as Netflix has done.

In the retail industry, this trend is compounded by the influx of retail store closings in recent years: 2017 saw retailers close 102 million square feet of store space, followed by 155 million square feet in 2018.[51] That trend doesn't appear to be slowing down any time soon. B2C companies with a physical presence will need to figure out how to innovate and personalize in the "brick-and-mortar" space. As they experiment with personalization in their digital channels, they will discover that personalization is the path to differentiation in their physical channels, too.

Trends in other industries are advancing the need for personalization as well. Most financial institutions believe they are relationship-driven organizations, yet 79% of consumers consider their relationship with their bank to be transactional in nature.[52] In travel, consumers are cost-conscious and not particularly loyal when it comes to booking trips; as a result, online travel agencies (OTAs) generally compete on the basis of price. The world of media and publishing is overloaded with content of all types, so the industry is struggling to provide any level of differentiation to effectively engage and retain their readers and viewers. Companies across these and other industries are finding that providing a personalized customer experience allows them to develop better relationships with, and thereby foster the loyalty of, their customers.

Additionally, as often happens in the world of technology, just when you think you have something figured out, the landscape changes. The ability to access the internet via personal computer was a game-changer for the marketing industry; businesses that do not have some kind of internet presence today are considered an anachronism. Mobile devices changed the game again more than a decade ago, and most marketers are still trying to work out how to creatively incorporate mobile into their marketing strategies. In *The One-to-One Future*, Peppers and Rogers listed multiple ways that the fax machine could be used to reach consumers at the one-to-one level, but how many marketers are using the fax machine as a marketing channel today? If history tells us anything, it is that new channels to reach consumers will continue to be invented—and that older channels will be phased out.

Below are some new and emerging technologies and channels that may define the future of B2C marketing.

IN-STORE EXPERIENCES

As retailers continue to explore personalization in digital channels, they seek ways to tie the digital experience to the in-store experience. But it isn't easy. Even in situations where retailers have built robust profiles containing all relevant information for each shopper, they often can't recognize a shopper until she identifies herself at the register. At that point, the sales associate may be able to recommend an add-on product or two, but it's too late to deliver a true personalized shopping experience.[53]

This can only change once retailers invest in in-store technologies to close the gap between online and in-store personalization. These best practices will evolve over the next few years, but we have some clues about the direction in-store personalization will take.

Loyalty programs are playing a big role in the future of in-store personalization, as they give retailers the ability to recognize shoppers in the store. Starbucks is clearly a leader in this area. Its loyalty program offers discounts and facilitates mobile ordering and payment as incentives to drive customers to join. Then Starbucks uses the information it collects about each customer's food and drink preferences, store visit frequency, and more to offer incentives that encourage her to keep returning to a store.[54]

Recognizing the importance of personalization to the Starbucks business, Scott Maw, CFO and Executive Vice President at Starbucks, said in early 2018:

> *What we have driven over the past several years is significant growth and... almost all of our same-store sales growth from those customers that we have digital relationships with and those that are in our Starbucks Rewards program. They are growing their spending rate somewhere between mid- to high-single digits. So you are getting both revenue per customer growth and the number of customer growth... most of that growth is coming from personalization.*[55]

McDonalds has taken the concept of in-store personalization even further by acquiring a personalization software vendor in early 2019. It plans to use the technology to personalize its drive-thru menu in real time based on weather patterns, current in-store traffic, trending items, etc. Going forward, it may even integrate the technology into its in-store ordering kiosks and its mobile app. While as of this book's publish date we have yet to see what McDonalds will be able to achieve with its acquired technology, one thing is clear: personalizing the in-store experience is a top priority for the brand.[56]

A combination of all of these technologies and tactics—personalization tech, loyalty programs, mobile apps, email marketing, in-store kiosks, drive-thru menus, and more—are needed to deliver a personalized experience in the physical location. We'll see many more retailers explore unique combinations of these technologies over the next several years to provide better and more relevant experiences across channels.

FACIAL RECOGNITION

Facial recognition technology also has the potential to provide more personalized experiences for consumers in the physical world. The technology is everywhere these days. For example, you've probably noticed that Facebook can automatically tag your friends in your photos. That's just the beginning. Facial recognition is being used to catch shoplifters, to keep an eye on gamblers in casinos, and to spot fake passports.[57]

It is also being utilized by advertisers to deliver more personalized ad content and provide more interactive experiences in the real world. For example, GM leveraged facial recognition in a video billboard in a mall in Santa Monica to promote the GMC Acadia. A visible camera was able to detect how many people were standing in front of the ad, the genders of those people, whether there were children in the group, and the facial expressions of the viewers. With that information, the ad (containing a man who was interacting directly with the audience) played one of thirty creative and engaging videos in real time to highlight the features of the car.[58]

Beyond personalized advertising, facial recognition has vast implications for B2C marketers. For example, retailers could install responsive screens in their front windows that displayed merchandise digitally rather than physically, personalizing that content to an individual's visual demographics as he or she walked by (like a physical version of a personalized homepage). Within a store itself, a retailer could track a shopper's behaviors with a multitude of cameras to help determine intent—a physical version of the digital tracking we described in this book. That data could be added to her individual profile so the retailer could develop a full understanding of her interactions with the company and, in turn, use that data in future interactions across channels.

There's a lot of potential in facial recognition technology that we'll see B2C companies explore more in the coming years.

NATURAL LANGUAGE PROCESSING

Natural Language Processing (NLP) has been defined as "a way for computers to analyze, understand, and derive meaning from human language in a smart and useful way."[59] It is not just about machines understanding language: it is about understanding how humans communicate in the real world so that machines can respond as a human would. Amazon's Alexa and Apple's Siri are two examples of NLP in action. We mentioned NLP in Chapter 2 as something that can be leveraged for personalization within one type of advanced algorithm. But more broadly, NLP has the potential to transform how marketers interact with consumers.

In the future, NLP will be more widely used on websites and apps to provide the type of service that a consumer could previously only receive from a fellow human in a store, on the phone or via online chat. A shopper could ask a chatbot on the site a question about what products are right for him based on his specific circumstances.[60] The chatbot can then provide answers to his questions via NLP without the need to involve an actual human.[61] With this approach, the shopper may feel more confident about his selection and be more likely to buy.

Retailers have certainly already begun to experiment with this type of technology. You may have heard of outdoor apparel brand The North Face's usage of IBM's Watson technology on its website several years ago. The North Face website provided the ability for shoppers to enter details about what they were looking for and what conditions they were planning to face. Watson then asked follow-up questions, as a human would do, to ultimately recommend appropriate products to meet each shopper's unique preferences and climate conditions—emulating the experience a shopper receives in a store from knowledgeable store associates.[62]

There is also potential for NLP to help consumers bridge the gap between the digital and physical worlds. Consumers could leverage NLP in a retailer's mobile app while in a store to ask questions (and receive answers) about where to find what they're looking for.[63] This could help speed up shopping trips for consumers and appeal to those who would rather accomplish the task on their own without speaking to an in-store associate.

In short, NLP will increasingly be used to simulate human-to-human interactions and to provide better, more personalized customer service across channels.

THE INTERNET OF THINGS

If you are like many consumers, you have incorporated "smart" appliances into your home. Maybe you have a smart thermostat, like Alphabet's Nest, that you can control from your phone. You may have a smart speaker, such as Amazon Echo or Google Home, that you can use to control various fixtures in your house (such as lights or fans). You may have an alarm system that you can control from your phone. Your stove might be WiFi enabled. You might even be able to view the inside of your refrigerator with a camera while you're in the grocery store.[64]

All of these devices can collect data on your usage. Your speaker knows what music you have asked it to play, what you have searched for, and how many times you have turned the lights on and off in a certain room. The alarm system knows how often you set it and how long you're away from the house. Your thermostat knows your heating and cooling preferences.

Imagine a world in which your house could use all of this data to build a single, unified profile for you. This data could be used to understand whether you're a regular traveler, whether your home contains small children, how environmentally conscious your household is, how often you and your family cook at home, and much more. Imagine that in this world, your house can make recommendations based on what may be relevant to you. For example, it could send you email recommendations of foods you may like to stock that you've not purchased in a while. It could recommend recipes you may like based on your food preferences and how frequently you cook. It could suggest energy efficient light bulbs. Your house could use the data it collects about you to make your life easier. And, if privacy were not a concern (more on that later), this information could be accessible to other marketers to make your life outside the home more relevant, too.

CARS

We all know that we interact with a number of screens (mobile phones, laptops, smart watches, etc.) every day. But one screen you may not think about is located in your car.

Most new cars sold today have some sort of screen in the dashboard, and some even have "heads up displays" that the driver can see directly ahead of her. With all the time commuters spend in the car every day, the car screen holds immense potential for marketers.

Car manufacturers and the big tech players are still working out who owns these screens. Apple CarPlay and Android Auto already exist to bring vehicles into the Apple and Google ecosystems, but some car manufacturers are trying to retain control over the screen by introducing their own cloud platforms.[65] This struggle over the car screen will certainly continue over the next few years, and the outcome will determine how the screen will be used as a marketing channel.

In addition to adding another screen to our lives, some cars today collect a lot of data on their drivers and their usage. For instance, Tesla collects data on each car's speed history, odometer information, air bag deployment, battery charging history, and more. It even collects videos of accidents.[66] Could data about who is driving the car and how the car has been driven be combined with location data and used for marketing in the future? Could we ever get to the point where billboards on highways are personalized to those driving by them? Might radio ads be tailored to the areas a person is driving through? These imaginings don't fall that far outside the realm of possibility.

Of course, we are not likely to encounter some of these predictions in the immediate future. While consumers are typically comfortable allowing their devices to collect data on them to improve their experiences with the devices themselves, it is unlikely that they will be comfortable with those devices sharing that data with other companies for advertising purposes. But there are so many different channels capturing data today, and technology is improving at such a rapid rate, that it is not unrealistic to think that one day the world we interact with will be completely personalized.

THE FUTURE OF B2B

When B2B products and services are sold through a salesperson, the sales process can be easy to personalize: the sales rep can leverage all he or she knows about the prospect to guide conversations and provide personalized recommendations. And, of course, sales teams can leverage digital data on these prospects to further individualize the interactions (as we described in Chapter 3).

But not all B2B sales interactions occur between a customer and a salesperson. Some B2B products and services are sold online. And even for products that are not sold online, today's B2B buyers conduct substantial research before reaching out to the company to see a demo or to speak to a salesperson.[67] B2B marketers, therefore, need to provide the best experiences possible in the digital world.

B2B marketers have traditionally been slower to adopt digital personalization than their B2C counterparts. But they are catching up! B2B marketers are exploring digital tactics that have been employed primarily by B2C marketers—particularly machine-learning personalization—but in a way that is uniquely theirs. B2B marketers already understand that their buyers are consumers, too, and they recognize that consumer expectations are being set by the Netflixes of the world. Generally content-marketing-focused versus ecommerce-driven, B2B companies understand the value of engaging their prospects with personalized content. They also recognize that buying decisions are most often made at the account, rather than the individual, level. The future of B2B marketing and personalization will rely on data to better understand accounts and the individuals within them to provide more relevant experiences.

INBOUND MARKETING

Personalization can play a key role in converting more visitors to leads on a B2B website. This applies to organizations employing an inbound marketing strategy, which is the practice of attracting and engaging audiences on the basis of search-optimized content and online ads—and then capturing their contact information in exchange for premium content assets like eBooks and webinars, product demonstrations or free trials. Such contact information is used for ongoing nurture marketing and/or passed on to the sales team for pursuit. With this approach, personalization is used to provide the most relevant content and experiences to prospects to ensure that they do, in fact, find enough value that they "convert" and provide their contact information.

ACCOUNT-BASED MARKETING (ABM)

While inbound marketing remains valuable for many companies, the future of B2B marketing for others is in account-based marketing (ABM). With ABM, a marketer's focus is on engaging individuals within target accounts, industries or sub-industries. Marketers that adopt a pure ABM strategy often have a product with a higher selling price, a longer sales cycle, and a narrower applicability to certain companies. As opposed to a pure inbound marketing strategy, which is ideal for an inside sales team or an e-commerce approach, ABM strategies are generally preferred by field sales-focused organizations. Many companies adopt a mix of both inbound and ABM strategies, falling somewhere in between the two ends of the spectrum. They may use inbound marketing to capture leads for smaller deals while targeting larger accounts using ABM techniques.

ABM will be implemented more and more by marketers when it makes sense to do so—predominantly by those who are focused on reaching target accounts in the digital world (and ensuring that each account receives relevant content and messages that catch their attention). Thus, the future of B2B personalization will be in finding the right data sources and the right tactics to understand and reach these target accounts in a scalable way.

UNGATED CONTENT

In recent years, in light of a glut of B2B company-supplied content, prospects have become more reluctant to provide their contact details early in their research efforts. As such, more and more companies, especially those pursuing an ABM strategy, have adopted a practice of "ungating" their content to drive greater awareness for their company's brand and adjust to the changing B2B buyer behavior.

Once barriers to content consumption are removed, prospects can quickly and easily navigate through a company's content library to find answers to their questions and learn more about the company's products or services. They no longer need to assess whether they will receive enough value from the content to justify giving up their contact information. This is objectively a better experience.

However, it presents a challenge for demand generation marketers who are tasked with generating leads. How do you capture leads to pass to the sales team if you don't require contact information? After relying on gated content to fuel their demand gen programs for the last decade or more, they need to figure out what comes next. For tech-savvy organizations, particularly those with a best-in-breed personalization solution, the answer is in remembering return visitors and tracking people without required form fills each time.

For those now relying on an ABM strategy, the effects of ungating may be limited. These companies do not need to capture the contact information of everyone who visits their sites—just those visitors from target accounts.

Even those who continue to operate traditional inbound marketing strategies may not notice a dramatic impact due to the decreasing quality of their lead data in recent years. Within our own data at Evergage before we ungated our content, a quarter of leads who filled out eBook forms were classified as "bad data" (meaning 25% of those who completed a form did so with fake or inaccurate information). Another 30% of leads were classified as "not a fit"—they didn't meet our qualification criteria to pursue. In addition, a large number of leads were "not interested," "unresponsive," or fell into other buckets that indicated they weren't good leads. It no longer made sense to require downloaders to fill out a form to access our content if we did not find the information valuable or usable.

Going forward, demand gen marketers will need to identify other ways to drive leads into the funnel, including how to identify visitors on the site when they can't fill out endless forms—potentially making use of some of the technology we have described in this book.

THIRD-PARTY INTENT DATA

One challenge facing both inbound and account-based marketing teams is that there is a lot of trial and error involved in the process. Which leads generated from inbound marketing efforts are valuable and worth further investment? Which tactics produce the best leads? Which accounts are worth dedicating time and budget to with account-based marketing tactics? Typically, answering these questions involves testing different approaches to find the optimal strategies.

An emerging category of vendors for B2B marketers are those providing "third-party intent" data (also called "B2B buyer intent data").[68] This refers to information on accounts and even individuals that, based on their behavior on the web (site/pages visited, content downloaded, ads engaged with, etc.), are found to be demonstrating interest in certain topics or solution areas which could indicate a potential fit for a company's products or services. Many of these vendors also provide sales intelligence capabilities that leverage predictive modeling to analyze a company's historical lead and opportunity data in order to identify and score prospects to identify ideal customers.[69] This approach takes some of the guesswork out of lead scoring and improves segmentation, targeting and sales follow-up.

In the future, this predictive style of B2B marketing will become more popular and will require more data-driven marketing professionals to manage it. This is also where a CDP will be valuable. These marketers will be responsible for identifying, integrating and managing all the data sources needed to run successful lead generation and account-based marketing programs. They will also leverage AI technologies to pull actionable insights from that data and execute more effective cross-channel personalization.

DEMAND UNITS

As they become more advanced in their targeting, B2B marketers will evolve beyond targeting accounts to targeting *demand units*. SiriusDecisions defines the demand unit as the group within the account specifically tasked with addressing a need. SiriusDecisions says that the "buyer, needs and solution must match for a demand unit to exist."[70] Essentially, ABM is not just about targeting companies that fit the profile your team has defined; it is about finding those companies that have also identified that they have "pain" around what your product or solution addresses. Recognizing those companies online requires much more precise targeting and must leverage first-party and third-party intent monitoring, advanced segmentation and more.

To achieve success in the future, B2B marketers must become experts not only in their buyers' pain points, but also in how to leverage data and technology to recognize which buying groups within accounts are actually experiencing those pain points and researching solutions to address them right now.

THE FUTURE OF ENGAGEMENT

In the near future, personalization will move beyond just selecting the most relevant experience for each person *within each channel*, to picking the *best channel* to engage each person in the first place. Will each of your SaaS customers be more likely to react to your announcement of a new feature if you communicate it via email, push notification, text message or in-app message? Will each shopper respond to your requests to take a survey via an infobar on your site or an ad on Facebook? These are the questions that marketers have today, and the technology will certainly exist in the future to answer them.

We're not big fans of the phrase "right message, right place, right time" because it's become a marketing cliché—and we believe no technology has been able to truly deliver on the "right place" aspect of this promise to date. But that will soon change, as the most innovative machine learning-driven personalization technologies will be able to understand each person's levels of engagement with each channel over time and use that knowledge to predict their likelihood to engage with particular messages in those channels.

Only when this is possible will we be able to fully deliver on the "right message, right place, right time" promise.

THE FUTURE OF THE TECHNOLOGY LANDSCAPE

Selecting the best mix of technologies to execute a marketing strategy has never been more difficult. (Recall that in Chapter 6, we noted that the number of martech solutions has surpassed 7,000.) As marketers attempt to bring together more data sources to reach more consumers and business buyers across multiple channels, they are going to become frustrated by the siloed nature of these technologies. We will see a trend of marketers looking to do more with fewer solutions (i.e., choosing fully featured platforms over one-off point solutions). The martech industry will likely respond to these pressures with continued product development investments and more mergers and acquisitions.

Of course, there will never be a single solution that marketers can use to address all of their needs and drive all of their activities. Many solutions, such as CRM and email marketing platforms, are deeply ingrained in the daily workflows of marketing teams. But we are starting to see the customer data platform emerge as the latest cornerstone martech solution (particularly because it collects and stores a massive amount of digital data, interprets it and makes it available for use across channels and other systems). Every new technology a company adopts must easily and seamlessly integrate with the many other martech products that exist and that will continue to be adopted. In short, to create a seamless customer experience, no piece of technology can be an island.

THE FUTURE OF PRIVACY

Given all that we have described about the future of personalization, we also need to talk about privacy. Since the early days of digital personalization, the marketing world has been rightly concerned about the proper and ethical use of customer and prospect data. Privacy concerns have grown in recent years as laws and regulations have been enacted to protect consumers' personal information. The most notable of these is the European Union's General Data Protection Regulation (GDPR), enacted in 2018, that gives EU citizens the right to control how they are tracked online—whether the company they interact with is based inside the EU or not. The US state of California passed a similar version of the regulation shortly after GDPR went into effect.[71]

While privacy should have always been a top priority for marketers, laws like these are requiring marketers to take privacy very seriously.

But prioritizing privacy doesn't mean avoiding personalization. Today, consumers recognize that brands are collecting their information. They are generally comfortable with this arrangement, particularly when they believe that they are also benefiting. In a study by Microsoft, 54% of respondents indicated that they "expect brands to really know and understand them as people, and for communications to be tailored to their values and preferences."[72] To enjoy this level of personalization, they recognize that they need to share their data. But they also want brands to be transparent about data collection. The study found that 83% of consumers expect brands and advertisers to ask for their permission before they use their digital information.[73]

In another study by Magnetic, 60% of respondents were comfortable with having their shopping interests and behaviors used by retailers to expedite their shopping experiences on the site, while 58% believed that the data would provide them with a better overall experience.[74] Thus, a good rule of thumb is that if consumer data is being sold or will be used in unexpected ways, consumers want the ability to provide consent. At the same time, they're generally comfortable with a company using their data to provide a better experience with that company.

The best approach to providing personalization to your customers, prospects or shoppers is to focus on improving the individual's overall experience. We always caution that it is not a good idea to personalize simply for the sake of personalization. Reminding someone that you know his name, location and past purchases across channels without providing any value can certainly come across as "creepy." What is most important—both because it is the right thing to do and because it is best for your business in the long run—is that you add value for each visitor and customer. You always want to be looking to use your customers' data to genuinely help them. And, of course, you should always obey the law.

Outside of legal requirements, what is appropriate will vary greatly from industry to industry and from business to business. For example, a fashion retailer can provide a valuable experience to its loyal shoppers with obvious personalization. Shoppers in the loyalty program could be greeted by name across the site and given access to a personalized boutique with products relevant to their stated or inferred preferences. But that type of obvious personalization might not be appropriate for a financial services site, for example. In that case, the site should subtly surface content based on a visitor's lifecycle stage or past behavior. The person will probably not recognize that any personalization is taking place, but should be able to find helpful content more quickly and easily.

In the future, as marketers seamlessly blend subtle personalization with intentional customization, consumer control will play a greater role in personalized experiences. For example, today Amazon provides the ability to remove purchases from data used to determine recommendations across the site. Going forward, more and more both B2B and B2C companies will offer individuals the opportunity to control which aspects of their profile will and won't be used for a better experience. While the purpose of personalization is to provide more relevant experiences to individuals without requiring them to take any action, as personalization evolves, it will be more of a partnership between companies and consumers.

THE FUTURE OF MACHINE LEARNING

In Chapter 2, we discussed machine-learning algorithms and how they power personalized experiences. We described that the way to customize your own algorithms is to start with one or more base algorithms and then layer in filters, boosters and variations to make them work for your organization and current needs. This is a great way for marketers or other business users without data science experience to control their own machine-learning algorithms.

In the future, we expect an evolution in the way marketers leverage machine learning. There are two main types of machine learning: traditional machine learning and deep learning. Traditional machine learning allows you to train an algorithm with labeled or structured data to learn and react in a certain way. When you have a specific problem you would like to solve or a question you would like to answer, you feed data to a machine-learning algorithm to help it learn how to solve that problem. Most of what we have described in this book is traditional machine learning.

Deep learning, on the other hand, is much more complicated. It leverages what is essentially a group of algorithms, called artificial neural networks, that attempt to solve problems as a human would. One of the most common examples of deep learning is facial recognition. The ability to analyze and recognize a face is complex, and a human cannot explain to a machine which elements of the face are important. There are a number of different problems to solve before an algorithm can identify a face. At the most basic level, it needs to be able to identify which part of a photo contains a face, pull out relevant facial features and match them to a network of other faces. Deep learning is required to solve this problem.

Going forward, deep learning that emulates the way humans interact with other humans will increasingly be used in digital personalization. The specifics of what that looks like remain to be seen, but we're looking forward to witnessing the evolution of machine learning in customer experiences!

Another development we anticipate is that machine learning personalization will have a significant impact on the needs and functions of content management systems (CMSs). Today, organizations typically design and deploy their website pages via a CMS. Sometimes, they will use rule-based personalization (leveraging features of the CMS or a separate personalization solution) to modify those pages for certain audiences. But imagine a world where *each page* of the website is dynamically created for each visitor, personalized to his or her preferences, in real time. In that world, driven by machine learning, the personalization engine would be used to present a different version of the website to each person, and the CMS would be used largely for the storage of content and images. It may seem a little futuristic, but this type of full-site, completely dynamic personalization is where we're headed.

MACHINE LEARNING–TAKING PERSONALIZATION TO THE NEXT LEVEL

Personalization sure has come a long way since the 1990s. Here's a quick recap of the major developments:

Surface-level to in-depth data: The data we can leverage for personalization has evolved dramatically over the decades. In the past, the best data we had available for web personalization was what a person had clicked on. Today, you can monitor a person's level of engagement with each page, compare it to his level of engagement across other pages, and leverage the context of the page itself to uncover his preferences, affinities and intent on your site. You can also combine behavioral data with data from a multitude of other sources within a CDP to build a complete picture of individuals and accounts.

Segment-based to true one-to-one targeting: The in-depth data required of true one-to-one, personalized communication is critical for powering machine learning. With machine learning, you can synthesize all the information you have available to identify the best, most relevant experience for each individual in a scalable way. While segment-based communication (the only type of web personalization Peppers and Rogers highlighted) continues to provide value, the future is in machine learning.

"Next time" to "real-time" decisioning: Advancements in data processing have dramatically improved personalization, allowing personalization engines to collect data in the moment, combine it with historical data, and deliver the most relevant experiences in real time. The possibility was beyond Peppers and Rogers' imagination in the mid-1990s, and it is still something that marketers struggle with today. But the importance of delivering personalization in real time cannot be overstated. In today's fast-moving world, waiting for someone to engage with your brand at a later date is a risk that most marketers should not be willing to take.

Siloed channels to integrated experiences: When developing personalization plans, it is easy for marketers to view each of their channels in isolation or even to view various pages of their websites as separate from the overall site experience. But today we have the ability to be more intentional with our personalization strategies. We can create integrated experiences that show customers that we know them as individuals across channels and contexts. It is more than adding an infobar to a mobile app or a row of product recommendations on a site's homepage. These are just pieces of a broader strategy. When Peppers and Rogers explained personalizing a CTA button for a chat room in 1994, they certainly did not have these kinds of integrated experiences in mind: the technology to implement a complete cross-channel personalization strategy at the one-to-one level did not exist.

––––––––––

It should be obvious at this point that the future of one-to-one personalization rests with machine learning. Machine learning has transformed the way marketers can interact with their shoppers, prospects and customers. Technology has evolved to allow marketers to collect and act on vast amounts of customer data in a scalable way to create tailored experiences for individuals and companies across channels.

It should also be clear from this book that we're headed in the direction of increasing personalization. This is not just because we *can* provide personalized experiences. It is because we *must* provide those experiences. Think about the number of messages competing for your attention every day. You probably get more emails than you would ever care to read. You hear and see ads everywhere. You can't keep up with all the different TV shows you could possibly watch. When you search for something on the web, you could never sift through every result. Now more than ever, marketers *have to* surface information relevant to the individual if they want to catch and keep the attention of both consumers and business buyers.

As a consumer yourself, think about the types of experiences *you* would like to have. When you find yourself on a website you've never visited before, how can that site capture your attention and prove that it's relevant to you? When you receive emails in your inbox, what would pique your interest enough to want to open them and click through? Which online ads would truly capture your attention? What would show you that a company you're loyal to knows you and appreciates your business?

Now think about how you can apply this perspective to your job as a marketer. How can you show your shoppers, visitors, prospects or customers that you truly know them, or that a particular product or service is right for them? How can you cut through all the noise in the market to deliver unique experiences that speak to each individual?

These are the questions that marketers will be asking themselves for years to come. The future of marketing is personalized. It is up to you, right now, to make sure that the future of your company's communications is personalized too.

CHAPTER 9 ENDNOTES

47. Don Peppers and Martha Rogers, The One to One Future, (New York: Doubleday, 1993), p. 339.

48. Frank Pallotta, "Netflix added record number of subscribers, but warns of tougher times ahead," CNN, Apr 2019, https://www.cnn.com/2019/04/16/media/netflix-earnings-2019-first-quarter/index.html.

49. Lara O'Reilly, "Netflix lifted the lid on how the algorithm that recommends you titles to watch actually works," Business Insider, Feb 2016, http://www.businessinsider.com/how-the-netflix-recommendation-algorithm-works-2016-2.

50. Ibid.

51. Hayley Peterson, "More than 7,000 stores are closing in 2019 as the retail apocalypse drags on — here's the full list," Business Insider, May 2019, https://www.businessinsider.com/stores-closing-in-2019-list-2019-3.

52. Accenture Consulting, "2016 North America Consumer Digital Banking Survey," 2016, https://www.accenture.com/t20160609T222453__w__/us-en/_acnmedia/PDF-22/Accenture-2016-North-America-Consumer-Digital-Banking-Survey.pdf.

53. Glenn Taylor, "Despite Push For Personalization, Just 18% Of Retailers Identify Shoppers In-Store," Retail Touchpoints, Dec 2018, https://www.retailtouchpoints.com/features/trend-watch/despite-push-for-personalization-just-18-of-retailers-identify-shoppers-in-store.

54. Mark Hamstra, "Restaurants Play Catch-Up with Data Analytics to Personalize the Fast-Food Experience," U.S. Chamber of Commerce, Apr 2019, https://www.uschamber.com/co/good-company/launch-pad/personalized-fast-food-experiences.

55. Jim Tierney, "Starbucks Understands That Personalization Drives Brand Loyalty," Loyalty360.com, Mar 2018, https://loyalty360.org/content-gallery/daily-news/starbucks-understands-that-personalization-drives.

56. Anthony Ha, "McDonalds is acquiring Dynamic Yield to create a more customized drive-thru," Techcrunch.com, Apr 2019, https://techcrunch.com/2019/03/25/mcdonalds-acquires-dynamic-yield/.

57. Molly Reynolds, "How Facial Recognition is Shaping the Future of Marketing Innovation," Inc.com, Feb 2017, https://www.inc.com/molly-reynolds/how-facial-recognition-is-shaping-the-future-of-marketing-innovation.html.

58. PR Web, "Responsive Facial Recognition Technology Redefines Customer Engagement for GMC Acadia," Sep 2016, http://www.prweb.com/releases/2016/09/prweb13710895.htm.

59. Algorithmia, "Introduction to Natural Language Processing (NLP) 2016," Aug 2016, https://blog.algorithmia.com/introduction-natural-language-processing-nlp/.

60. Mantas Malukas, "AI Chatbots: An Evolving Trend in Brand Marketing,"

Nichehunt.com, Jul 2017, https://nichehunt.com/
chatbots-an-evolving-trend-in-brand-marketing/.

61. Margaux, Mengebier, "How Natural Language Processing & Artificial
Intelligence are Changing Ecommerce," CentricDigital.com, Dec 2016, https://
centricdigital.com/blog/artificial-intelligence/
how-natural-language-process-artificial-intelligence-are-changing-ecommerce/.

62. The North Face, Fluid, and IBM, "The North Face, IBM and Fluid Launch
New Interactive Shopping Experience using Artificial Intelligence (AI)," Prnewsire.
com, Dec 2015, https://www.prnewswire.com/news-releases/the-north-face-ibm-
and-fluid-launch-new-interactive-shopping-experience-using-artificial-intelli-
gence-ai-300192085.html.

63. Margaux, Mengebier, "How Natural Language Processing & Artificial
Intelligence are Changing Ecommerce," CentricDigital.com, Dec 2016, https://
centricdigital.com/blog/artificial-intelligence/
how-natural-language-process-artificial-intelligence-are-changing-ecommerce/.

64. Matt Burgess, "You can now talk to your Samsung fridge," Wired.co.uk, Feb
2017, http://www.wired.co.uk/article/samsung-family-hub-2-smart-fridge.

65. Ben Algaze, "The Digital Multi-Screen Experience: Coming Soon to a Car Near
You," Extremetech.com, Jan 2018, https://www.extremetech.com/
extreme/262092-digital-multi-screen-experience-coming-soon-car-near.

66. Tesla, "Customer Privacy Policy," 2017, https://www.tesla.com/about/legal.

67. Megan Heuer, "Three Myths of the '67 Percent' Statistic," SiriusDecisions, Jul
2013, https://www.siriusdecisions.com/blog/three-myths-of-the-67-percent-statistic.

68. Amy Koski, "Definition: B2B Buyer Intent Data," Aberdeen, Feb 2019, https://
www.aberdeen.com/featured/blog-definition-b2b-purchase-intent-data/.

69. Todd Berkowitz, "The Evolution of the Predictive B2B Marketing Analytics
Space," Gartner, Apr 2018, https://blogs.gartner.com/
todd-berkowitz/04292018_the-evolution-of-the-predictive-b2b-marketing-analytics-
space/.

70. Jessica Lillian, "Meet the Newest SiriusDecisions Demand Waterfall!"
SiriusDecisions, May 2017, https://www.siriusdecisions.com/blog/
meetthenewestsiriusdecisionsdemandwaterfall.

71. Mark G. McCreary, "The California Consumer Privacy Act: What You Need to
Know," Law.com, Dec 2018, https://www.law.com/njlawjournal/2018/12/01/
the-california-consumer-privacy-act-what-you-need-to-
know/?slreturn=20190502173152.

72. Greg Sterling, "Survey: 99 Percent Of Consumers Will Share Personal Info For
Rewards, But Want Brands To Ask Permission," Marketingland.com, Jun 2015,
http://marketingland.com/
survey-99-percent-of-consumers-will-share-personal-info-for-rewards-also-want-

brands-to-ask-permission-130786.

73. Ibid.

74. Sterling, Greg. "Consumers Want Personalization, But Retailers Just Can't Seem To Deliver." Marketingland.com. Sep 2015, http://marketingland.com/consumers-want-personalization-but-retailers-just-cant-seem-to-deliver-144021.